HELL IN FOUR RIVERS

Memoirs of Zlatomir Šarić

A Tale of War and Betrayal in Old Yugoslavia

Zlatomir Saric

First Edition 2016
MMXVI

Library of Congress
Cataloging-in-Publication Data

Šarić, Zlatomir
Title 1. Bosnia. 2. Yugoslavia. 3. War. 4. Prisoners of Yugoslavia War

ISBN-13: 9781523649402
ISBN-10: 1523649402

Printed in the United States of America

Passages in Italics are direct quotes from Zlatomir Šarić's journal that he memorized during his capture and then wrote down after his release from the prisons.

DEDICATIONS
This book is dedicated in loving memory to: All patriots during the 1991 to 1995 war in Bosnia and the war prisoners and the children who continued to be injured and killed in the minefields left over from the war.

As Narrated by Zlatomir Šarić
Written from Zlatomir Šarić's Journal and Narratives by Janice Brunson 2015
Rewritten from Zlatomir Šarić's further Narratives and his Journal by Sharon Willow-Smith 2016

PROLOGUE

When Zlatomir, the last surviving child born into the Šarić family came into this world, his father joked that any name for a boy was already in use by his other sons so he coined one. 'Zlato' means gold in the Bosnian language and 'mir' means piece, hence gold piece. Out of 13 children, he was treasured as the last of nine children that survived birth. This was the gift his father gave to his last son.

Dubbed the 'Jerusalem of the Balkans,' Sarajevo is celebrated for classical beauty. It lies alongside the powerful Miljacka in a scenic valley guarded by towering Dinaric Alps. It is a modern city, a cultural social center and a major economic force in Europe. At the turn of the century the first electric tram service in Europe began in Sarajevo. In 1984 the city received worldwide recognition as host of the Fourteenth Winter Olympics. In 2012 Sarajevo was named a 'European Capital of Culture,' the only city to be nominated that is not a member of the European Union. It is also a city rich in religious tolerance. People of diverse religious backgrounds have lived side by side as neighbors for centuries.

When Zlatomir was a teen and for years thereafter, he visited relatives living in this 'Balkan Jerusalem,' his brothers, their families and numerous cousins. He fondly recalls a magical city ringing with music and people laughing. Downtown Sarajevo springs into life in the evenings when huge crowds stroll along the broad

Marshall Tito Boulevard greeting friends and strangers alike and toasting one another over glasses of beer or homemade plum brandy called slivovitza. Zlatomir would meet up with friends in Sarajevo and while away long evenings, picking up girls, dancing and learning to drink like an adult.

Zlatomir Šarić's homeland is Bosnia and it is considered by many as one of the most beautiful regions in Eastern Europe. The country is graced with countless scenes suitable for a lovely postcard. There are forests of towering firs a century or more old and waterways teeming with plump fish on an eastern swim to the Adriatic Sea. Ancient bridges span rivers and streams. Cobblestone lanes meander through old settlements with red-tiled roofs. Church spires gracefully break the horizon. After winter snows melt, summer orchards spring into bloom, producing prodigious amounts of ripe fruit. Flower blooms along the roadways and blanket surrounding hills and peaks. At every corner there is a small café or coffee house where Bosnian men gather most evenings for the favored pastime, visiting over cups of thick Turkish coffee.

Throughout Europe, Bosnians are noted for a lively wit and warm character. In a group they are generally relaxed and not easily riled. They have lived peacefully for generations in tranquil settings except during the periods of the Great Wars in the Twentieth Century. Zlatomir is no exception. He is tall with a wild head of hair, now snow white, reminiscent of the twentieth century genius Einstein. He is a handsome man with an easy warm smile in his unlined face and a mischievous twinkle in his eyes. His thick accent only adds to his gregarious charm. Old world manners come naturally to him by quickly opening doors for women and engaging you with lively, intelligent conversation. Before you know it he has learned more about you than one expected to reveal.

But look more deeply and there is something more. Every man in the coffee bar, the one who is telling a funny story or the man who is laughing, knows at least another who a short time ago died violently in a recent skirmish of war. It may have been a relative, a close friend or a mere acquaintance, a man who was shot, blown apart or buried alive. This man has also likely killed another, somebody who was trying to kill him. Such veterans also know many others who were forced from their homes abandoning everything they had spent a lifetime amassing. At an age when most men customarily rest on previous achievements, these men had to start over in their middle years, forced to rebuild their lives in foreign countries, leaving behind family, friends, their education, language and way of life.

In the years since the war, little has been written by the average Bosnian soldier caught up in a bloody conflict that ravaged the country for nearly four years, from early 1992 to late 1995. This is the story of one man, his hard experience in a vicious fight that was not of his making, a cunning duplicity that caught him and countless others up in desperate prison camps, and eventual exile from a homeland he loved. He left behind a large family that included a mother and his brothers and sisters.

Zlatomir is a private man. He is a man who is somewhat mysterious, cloaked in secrets from the past, a living reminder of a terrible time in old Yugoslavia, in the nation of Bosnia. It takes him a great deal of time to tell his story. He is reluctant to talk about harrowing moments, like the time when he and his brother Miro faced almost certain death when first arrested. If the subject arises Zlatomir quickly changes the subject. Perhaps this is a natural trait. More likely it is a defense he has mastered in response to an especially harsh lesson he learned when friends and neighbors of a lifetime turned on one another for seemingly little reason. In telling the story he jumps from one instance to another as his mind flits and he tells his story in various fragments.

In prison, Zlatomir memorized every detail he considered significant. He filed away memories by silently repeating the same facts to himself over and over again. He volunteered to work outside the barracks at every opportunity, performing such menial tasks as pulling weeds or collecting trash. The moments provided him quiet time when he memorized anything he considered important about the camp. He relied on word triggers to call up the names of individual guards and dates of significance. Whether he was raking the grounds or hauling garbage, he continuously muttered to himself committing to memory details of the dreadful ordeal. "I wanted to remember what happened. I didn't want to forget anything. I wanted to remember every detail."

Zlatomir began writing about the experience while waiting for an exit visa out of Yugoslavia. He jotted down his thoughts into a thick tablet. The pages quickly multiplied, growing into a makeshift manuscript. It was Zlatomir's intimate journal, a detailed and precise version of a treacherous time that this book is recorded from. Some twenty years later the journal assumed renewed importance when Zlatomir began to expand the original account into a fuller story. The project posed enormous challenges for him, including a precarious emotional journey into a dreadful past. Zlatomir had to dredge up from the past an experience because "it was so bad" he had carefully blocked it from his memory in order to start his new life in the United States. In the beginning he experienced a foreboding that eventually became mild depression for a brief period. "It was like revisiting hell," Zlatomir said, "a ruthless place filled with bile threats, harsh treatment and the screams of prisoners who were already half dead. The worst part was feeling helpless as relatives, friends and colleagues slowly deteriorated. Once strong men, they were slowly reduced to pitiful skeletons. Life slipped away by inches each day. Then the dying began. Indifferent prison guards who had known the prisoners from before the war, looked on with disinterest. They were now considered enemies."

In time, Zlatomir's feeling began to fade and recall was not nearly as intense, nor distressful as in the beginning. Horrifying details grew less vivid and eventually receding into manageable memory. Zlatomir began to tell the story in fragments, usually in response to a direct question. It became clear that his efforts to permanently erase the memories were in vain. His mind betrayed him. The memories remained clear and he eventually came to re-alize it was simply too significant an experience to ever be entirely forgotten. It is likely he will always live with the memories, some that continues to be vivid. When Zlatomir first started to recall the past, he grew tense and agitated. He was filled with despair. He had purposely ignored this part of his life until now, only speak-ing about it with close friends of similar experience. Once he be-gan his journey into yesteryear, he became depressed. Disturbing memories invaded his mind, "boomerangs" as he referred to the flashbacks that returned with a vengeance and without warning. He suffered nightmares at night, waking sweaty with a jolt from deep sleep. It was harrowing and he pondered whether or not to continue with the project because of the discomfort. He grew am-bivalent about the project, questioning whether or not to continue. Maybe it should be ended. He paused for day on end while gather-ing together coherent streams of thought in his mind. He wrestled with a decision for weeks. Finally he made a firm decision. "I have started this. Now it must be finished." He became more deter-mined than ever to complete his story. He is determined to tell his story from beginning to end.

CHAPTER ONE

Zlatomir is the last of nine surviving children born into the family over a period of two decades and had not yet been born at the time of either World War.

In the decades following World War II, the educational system remained virtually unchanged until it eventually functioned outside the mainstream of modern life. Students inadvertently contributed to the calamity. They were conditioned by upbringing and strict social boundaries. They rarely if ever challenged adult authority, even when it logically seemed to be in error. Teachers rank next to parents as ultimate figures of authority in authority, a situation that is not unique according to Zlatomir. He says that when threatened, people nearly always revert to easy explanations that offer the most promise of comfort and safety. Based on countless accounts in history, simple answers have always served as a coping mechanism for great numbers of people who are forced to confront evil by others.

Like all families then, the Šarić family sensed great danger in discussing controversy. They carefully monitored what was said, both at home and in public. When the family gathered around the long table for meals, they spoke quietly among themselves, maintaining a self-imposed silence on subjects that carried the threat of trouble. In the periods following the two great World Wars of 1917 and 1940, Bosnian families learned to carefully avoid controversy. Otherwise, they courted official sanction. The Šarić family was particularly protective of both Zlatomir and his three years older brother Miro. If by chance controversy did creep into conversations it is unlikely children would understand the full significance of the discussion.

Yugoslavia gained international recognition on July 13, 1922 at the Conference of Ambassadors in Paris. The country was named after the South Slavic peoples and constituted their first union, following centuries in which the territories had been part of the Ottoman Empire and Austria-Hungary. Renamed the Kingdom of Yugoslavia on October 3, 1929, it was invaded by the Axis powers on April 6, 1941. The Democratic Federal Yugoslavia was so proclaimed by the Partisan resistance in 1943. In 1944, the king recognized it as the legitimate government, but in November 1945 the monarchy was abolished. Yugoslavia was renamed the Federal People's Republic of Yugoslavia in 1946 when a communist government was established. It acquired the territories of Istra, Rijeka and Zadar from Italy. Partisan leader Josip Broz Tito ruled the country as president until his death in 1980. In 1963 the country was renamed again as the Socialist Federal Republic of Yugoslavia (SFRY). As a Federal Republic, Yugoslavs enjoyed unbridled prosperity until 1992. People lived the good life in an era that is referred to by international economists as an economic boon. For the first time, education was available to all and literacy dramatically increased. Medical care was free to all. Smaller families became the norm, the number of jobs doubled and people began living much longer, well into their seventies. New laws ensured greater personal freedom and rights for those who worked. The newly liberalized political system provided greater political policies equally favored both the east and the west, and when the Yugoslavian borders were open, tourism grew into a major industry. Those who could afford it took full advantage of the open borders and many traveled abroad for the first time. It was during this time that Zlatomir grew into an adult. He in the petroleum field. He married, divorced a dozen years later, and spent long evenings with friends at local outdoor cafés, and weekends camping and hiking in the beautiful hills and mountains that surround Čapljina.

People of Zlatomir's age, those who were born in the years following World War II, never suffered the hardship common to earlier generations of Yugoslavians. They never suffered the hardship and fear their parents survived during two world wars in the first half of the Twentieth Century. This later generation became the adults at the precise time Yugoslavia matured into a stable nation. They enjoyed the trappings of modernization and the fruits of prosperity. They were the first generation able to dream of the future and all of them fully expected to realize their dreams. The marked change was possible by a change of political leaders who had matured over the years and now understood that rapid development and expanded markets meant a new and better future. A new society had replaced the old.

This period is fondly recalled as the gilded age, a time of greater tolerance when everything seemed possible to the average Yugoslavian. Numerous small businesses like beauty shops and restaurants successfully opened in cities and towns throughout the country. Some five million peasants migrated from farms to the cities where they learned new skills for modern jobs. Workdays ended in mid-afternoon, providing ample leisure time for the traditional evening gatherings with family and friends. Those lucky enough to become adults now experienced life quite differently from earlier generations who far too often faced political instability and grinding poverty. Life was both pleasant and enjoyable for those who came later.

Zlatomir and his generation remained acutely mindful of the past. Although Zlatomir's parents rarely spoke of the hardships they endured, a sister who was thirteen years older than him told Zlatomir about a childhood that remained for her a vividly unhappy time. During the war and in the years immediately following, life was uncertain and filled with misery. Like many, she told him, their family often went hungry and during freezing winter months they were cold. Things worsened immediately after World War II, in 1948, when Zlatomir's father was arrested and briefly jailed for unspecified "partisan" activity. Zlatomir's mother, left alone with a number of small children, persevered the best she could. Her situation was common to many women then. Everyone suffered, including relatives, friends and neighbors. Two world wars had robbed many women of their husbands and lovers who were killed in battle. Others died without reason simply because there was not enough medicine or medical care available. Poor people burned their furniture to keep warm and when tables, chairs and bed rails were gone, they tore up floors and burned the wooden slats.

Aside from the stories, hardship did not impact Zlatomir or his friends. Nor, apparently, did it influence emerging leaders who neglected to draw from a collective past for use as a roadmap into the future. The results were disastrous. The disintegration of the new Yugoslavia began in the late 1980's when the center of power, the Communist Party, faltered and eventually dissolved in 1990. Inflation grew rampant, a staggering 3,000 percent a month. There was a simultaneous revival of nationalism. The nation's six semi-autonomous republics, SR Bosnia and Hercegovina, SR Croatia, SR Montenegro, SR Macedonia, SR Slovenia and SR Serbia. Serbia contained two Socialist Autonomous Provinces, Kosovo and Vojvodina, which after 1974 were largely equal to the other members of the federation. After an economic and political crisis in the 1980's and the rise of nationalism, Yugoslavia broke up along its republics' borders, at first into five countries leading to the Yugoslav Wars.

After the breakup, the republics of Serbia and Montenegro formed a reduced federation, the Federal Republic of Yugoslavia (FRY), which aspired to the status of sole legal successor to the SFRY, but the other former republics were opposed to these claims. Eventually, Serbia and Montenegro accepted the opinion of the Banister Arbitration Committee about shared succession.

After nearly a century of struggle, including surviving two bloody world wars, Yugoslavia had grown from a kingdom into a prosperous and stable republic. When the Kingdom of Serbs, Croats and Slovenes were founded in 1918, Yugo or South Slavia finally became a cohesive nation.

The war broke out when the new regimes tried to replace Yugoslav civilian and military forces. In August of 1990 Croatia attempted to replace police in the Serb populated Croat Krajina by force, the population first looked for refuge in the Yugoslavian Army barracks, while the army remained passive. The civilians' protests mark the beginning of the Yugoslav war that inflamed the region. Similarly, the attempt to replace Yugoslav frontier police by Slovenian police forces provoked regional armed conflicts, which finished with a minimal number of victims.

In Croatia, Serbian uprisings began in August of 1990 by blocking roads leading from the Dalmatian coast towards the interior almost a year before Croatian leadership made any move towards independence. These uprisings were, more or less discretely backed up by the Serb-dominated federal army (JNA).

The Serbs in Croatia proclaimed "Serb autonomous areas", later united into the Republic of Serb Krajina. The federal army tried to disarm the territorial defense forces of Slovenia, with the republics' local defense forces similar to the Home Guard, in 1990 but was not completely successful. Still Slovenia began to covertly import arms to replenish its armed forces.

Much later it was discovered that Croatia also embarked upon the illegal import of arms soon after the disarmament of the republics' armed forces by the federal army, mainly from Hungary. They were under constant surveillance, which produced a video of a secret meeting between the Croatian Defense Minister Martin Špegelj, and the two men were filmed by the Yugoslav counter-intelligence. Špegelj announced that they were at war with the army and gave instructions about arms smuggling as well as methods of dealing with the Yugoslav Army's officers stationed in Croatian cities. Serbia and JNA used this discovery of Croatian rearmament for propaganda purposes.

In the same month, the Army leaders met with the Presidency of Yugoslavia in an attempt to get them to declare a state of emergency, which would allow for the army to take control of the country. The army was seen as an arm of the Serbian government by that time so the consequence feared by the other republics was to be total Serbian domination of the union. The representatives of Serbia, Montenegro, Kosovo and Vojvodina voted for the decision, while all of the other republics, Croatia, Slovenia, Macedonia and Bosnia and Herzegovina voted against it. The tie delayed an escalation of conflicts, but not for long.

After the first multi-party election results, in the autumn of 1990, the republics of Slovenia and Croatia proposed transforming Yugoslavia into a loose confederation of six republics. With this proposal, the republics would have the right to self-determination. However, Bosnian Serb leader Slobodan Milošević rejected all such proposals, arguing that like Slovenes and Croats, the Serbs, mainly Croatian Serbs, should also have a right to self-determination.

Demonstrations were held against Milošević in Belgrade on March 9, 1991. The police and the military were deployed in the streets to restore order and killed two people. Late in March 1991, the Plitvice Lakes incident was one of the first sparks of open war in Croatia. The Yugoslav People's Army (JNA), whose superior officers were mainly of Serbian ethnicity, maintained an impression of being neutral but as time passed they got more and more involved in state politics.

Slovenia and then Croatia declared independence on June 25, 1991 and withdrew from the Yugoslavian Republic. The federal customs officers in Slovenia on the border crossings with Italy, Austria and Hungary just changed uniforms since most of them were local Slovenes. The next day the Federal Council ordered the army to take control of the "internationally recognized borders" which led to the Ten Day War. Based in barracks in Slovenia and Croatia, the Yugoslav People's Army forces attempted to carry out the task within the next 48 hours. But because of misinformation given to the Yugoslav Army conscripts that the Federation was under attack by foreign forces and the fact that the majority of them did not wish to engage in a war on the ground where they served their conscription, the Slovene territorial defense forces retook most of the posts within several days with only minimal loss of life on both sides.

The Austrian ORF TV network showed footage of three Yugoslavian soldiers surrendering to the territorial defense force before gunfire was heard and the troops were seen falling down. Although none were killed in the incident, it was viewed as a suspected incident of a war crime. There were however numerous cases of destruction of civilian property and civilian life by the Yugoslav People's Army which included houses and a church. A hanger and aircraft inside the hangar was bombarded, plus truck drivers on the road from Ljubljana to Zagreb and Austrian journalists at the Ljubljana Airport were killed.

Eventually a ceasefire was agreed upon. According to the Brioni Agreement, recognized by representatives of all republics, the international community pressured Slovenia and Croatia to place a three-month moratorium on their independence. During these three months the Yugoslav Army completed its pullout from Slovenia, but in Croatia a bloody war broke out in the autumn of 1991. Ethnic Serbs who had created their own state Republic of Serbian Krajina in heavily Serb populated regions, resisted the police forces of the Republic of Croatia who were trying to bring that breakaway region back under Croatian jurisdiction. There were some strategic places where the Yugoslav Army acted as a buffer zone, but in most areas it was protecting or aiding Serbs with resources and even manpower in their confrontation with the new Croatian army and their police force.

In September of 1991 the Republic of Macedonia also declared independence thus becoming the only former republic to gain sovereignty without resistance from the Belgrade based Yugoslav authorities. Five hundred United States soldiers were then deployed under the United Nations banner to monitor Macedonia's northern borders with the Republic of Serbia.

Bosnia followed soon thereafter when an overwhelming majority of Bosnians voted for forming a Serbian republic within the borders of Bosnia and Herzegovina and staying in a common state with Serbia and Montenegro in November of 1991.

Once Bosnia gained international recognition, events moved quickly. Serbian nationalists in the Bosnia government objected to independence and Bosnian Serb troops began to expand and increase attacks on small hamlets with renewed vigor. Although it is unlikely that the average citizen realized it at the time, the start of hostilities signaled the beginning of the end of Yugoslavia.

"We knew war was at the front door," Zlatomir recalled of his hometown Čapljina.

"It is ready to start but what can we do? We waited. We thought it would end nicely, that the United Nations would get involved and there

would be talks. But when the Serbs put guns all around in the hills, we knew it would be war. We just didn't know how horrible it was going to be."

CHAPTER TWO

As fighting grew ever closer to Čapljina, it became evident that it was only a matter of time before Zlatomir's hometown and the many small settlements nearby would be drawn into this infamous ring. Small towns like Slapovi and Kravice to the north and Klepci and Struge to the south were threatened and were vulnerable. During November of 1992 Zlatomir and several of his friends enlisted in the Croatian Army. They were more than ready to defend their hometown and fight together to do so.

Bosnian Serb leader Milošević was an ultra-extreme nationalist who clung to a misdirected dream he called 'Greater Serbia'. To achieve the dream, he needed to annex vast territories of land in Bosnia and make them Serbian. To accomplish this, Milošević needed support from Bosnian Serbs. First he captured full control of the Yugoslavian Army, then he undertook control of Bosnian's state broadcasting system, both radio and television airwaves. He swamped the airwaves with his own propaganda, vitriolic speeches aimed at inciting ancient animosities against Muslims.

The broadcasts by Milošević, were filled with distorted facts and outright lies, and he indulged in grotesque acts meant to create additional fear. In one instance he ordered Serbian corpses to be unearthed and the grisly remains be placed on public display. He called every Bosnian a murderer and warned that Muslims in Bosnia were intent on "jihad". Jihad, an Arabic word meaning holy war, carried untold terror among the frightened citizens.

The majority was stunned by Milošević's shocking announcements. They had never before paid a single moment of thought to the idea of holy war. Now they began to deeply worry about the prospect. Were Muslims, people who had previously been their friends, ready to attack those who were not Muslim?

Would people be murdered in their own beds? Would entire families die? People feared for their families, that they perhaps faced extermination by their neighbors.

It is highly doubtful that the secular Muslims of Bosnia ever conceived of such an attack. The message was a stunning surprise to everyone, including Muslims, who had never before given the topic a moment of thought. Most Bosnian Muslims were not religious and it is doubtful many of them could repeat the pillars of their faith, let alone describe the meaning of jihad.

Inconceivably, an identical campaign was underway in Africa, where Rwandan leaders incited Tutsi tribesman into killing neighboring Hutus that they labeled "cockroaches". In 1994, a million or so men, women and children were hacked to death by machete in little more than a month. Bosnians were Milošević's cockroaches and in his mind they too, needed to be exterminated.

Many saw Milošević's tirades as the rants of a disturbed man, but in time, those who were susceptible began to heed his message. They were people who were stuck in yesteryear, were poorly educated or were seeking revenge for past mistreatment or injustices. Misfits and criminals were warmed by the idea of war. To them it promised potential profits.

Other homegrown ultra nationalists joined Milošević in his tawdry campaign. Among them was Radovon Karadžić, a Bosnian Serb who had given the order to shoot on the Sarajevo peace rally. A psychiatrist by training, Karadžić was an amateur poet who authored the plan for ethnic cleansing, considered the worst atrocity in Europe since World War II. He insisted that bodies of dead Bosnians were little more than plastic dummies artfully arranged by Bosnians in search of sympathy.

Karadžić, known to be a gambler, remained on the lam for over a decade after the war, earning a living by practicing alternative medicine and issuing fake medical reports for those in search of early retirement or for criminals hoping to avoid punishment by pleading insanity. Described as a "mad man", he was among the world's most wanted men when finally arrested in July 2008. On trial in The Hague, Netherlands, in 2012, Karadžić denied all charges and told an astonished court that he was a "mild and tolerant man with great capacity to understand others," suggesting he deserves to be rewarded for all the good that he accomplished.

Bosnian Serb General Ratko Mladić, dubbed the butcher of Bosnia and the butcher of Srebrenica, had little regard for civilian casualties. He led the siege on Srebrenica that ended in the death of some 8,000 males between 12 to 77 years of age. He is responsible for bloody attacks on Sarajevo, including the one that killed the young medical student, Sauda Dilberović. Mladić's only daughter, Ana was also a medical student and rumored at the time to be in love with a Muslim. She committed suicide in early 1994 after reportedly learning of her father's war crimes. Mladić fled into hiding but was caught 16 years after the war ended and brought to trial in 2012 in The Hague where his angry tirades both cowered and insulted victims and court authorities.

Bosnian scholars have concluded that men like Karadžić and Mladić were able to remain undetected for years because they were hidden in an elaborate network of sympathizers, including police officers and members of the intelligence services in Bosnia, Serbia and Montenegro, as well as members of the Serbian Orthodox Church. The Church has long aligned itself with war criminals like Mladić, as well as a Croat Serb leader named Goran Hadžić who murdered hundreds and forced 28,000 from their homes. As recently as 2011, priests performed a eulogy in praise of a book by war criminal Milan Lukić who, together with a cousin, were convicted in 2009 for the "most terrible of crimes." Among other things, Lukić set fire to buildings filled with children, women and old men, burning them alive.

Zlatomir is convinced that such extreme nationalists directly influenced the violent nature of the war.

It was far worse than anyone could have ever thought possible or predicted, fought with a seemingly mindless fury. It was very bloody. People began to remember the past and the more they remembered, the more they wanted revenge. Terrible war. Stupid people!

Milošević's dream of an ethnically pure state for Serbians is eerily reminiscent of that from another era during which millions died in Germany. "Greater Serbia" was little more than a latter day Nazi idea, a perverted urge for a monolithic population devoid of all minorities. For a brief time Milošević was well on his way to the dream. By the summer of 1992, during a time of many casualties, Serbia had conquered nearly two thirds of Bosnia under Milošević's command.

The Bosnian War is both complex and confusing for many. It occurred in a part of Europe that few beyond the Balkans can fully appreciate or clearly understand. Many view the region as mysterious, a place filled with intrigue and dark passion. Neighboring nations refer to Bosnia as the "powder keg" of the Balkans, where leaders are prone to impulsive decisions. In the days leading up to war, a time filled with threats and insults between warring parties, western leaders, journalists and soldiers failed to grasp the Serbian strategy meant to achieve a "greater Serbia". The confusion led to flawed interpretation and conclusions that later proved disastrous. Essential background information and factual detail was inadvertently omitted and not included in western reports.

It was, for example, widely reported that the Bosnian War was the result of historical hatreds among a populace of enormous ethnic and religious divisions. People had lived in too small region for too long period of time. In reality, the average Bosnian paid scant attention to either history or ethnicity, paying only cursory attention to either issue. They knew neither provided a certain blueprint to the future. If anything, interest about the heritage of grandparents and parents were at an all time low. People simply were not concerned in any serious way about such things.

Bosnians were primarily concerned with routine matters that impact quality of life such as jobs with decent pay, stable homes, good education for children and retirement benefits. To attribute the cause of war to historical or ethnic differences are easy answers that are factually inaccurate. It defies imagination to think otherwise. Still, certain historians and political analysts maintain such theories and their positions continue to sway opinion, in spite of strong evidence to the contrary.

As time would prove, ethnic and religious differences, and a history filled with diversity among neighbors, did not cause the war. Diversity became the means by which unscrupulous political leaders were able to incite hostilities. They manipulated people into believing outlandish ideas about diversity, inciting them into dangerous prejudices that ultimately led to hard positions on either side. Politicians were successful in turning citizen against citizen. Leaders primarily concerned with their own trappings of success and wealth twisted the truth or outright lied. In an ironic twist, these leaders, unscrupulous men seemingly without conscience, manipulated rage. They convinced people that war was the only solution that could save them from disaster, the only acceptable stance.

The Bosnian War was a territorial conflict. The Bosnian Republic is sandwiched between two republics, Serbia to the east and Croatia to the west and north. Croatian and then Serbian troops attacked Bosnia, led by hungry men in search of new territory to expand their own territories. Bosnia did not at the time have an established army or a military tradition, and was not in position to defend itself.

When civil war erupted in 1991, Yugoslavia was recognized worldwide as a nation of strength and prosperity located in Europe. But during the disruption caused by civil war, Yugoslavia splintered into six separate republics. Each had its own leaders who coordinated efforts to create a united political front that had more power. But inherent weaknesses in the system surfaced with a vengeance once war erupted. Local leaders became suspicious of one another and grew distant.

Official communication channels broke down and lingering disputes led to instability that took an enormous toll on the entire political system.

Within a year, old Yugoslavia began to unravel and then quickly stopped operating as a functioning political system. Although the country had once been recognized and respected worldwide for decades, it began to implode. A unique governing system that had successfully functioned for years quickly disappeared without a trace. Central Europe was not the only region in the world then facing civil disruption that threatened entire populations. Rwanda in Central Africa attracted world attention when one million Rwandans murdered another million of their neighbors. In the former Soviet Union, by the government, upheavals in satellite republics like Georgia and Ukraine were squashed in bloody confrontations with the Russian military.

There are countless instances throughout history when friendly nations that had been close political allies grew into violent enemies over claims of territory, borders and political power. It is not a unique or uncommon phenomenon. There are examples since the beginning of man's history, throughout Europe, Asia and elsewhere. Bosnians, Croats and Serbs were simply the most recent actors caught up in a terrifying drama on a frightening world stage during the late 1980's.

The situation was perhaps more unsettling to people in Central Europe than elsewhere. Most Yugoslavians are very aware of their tumultuous history and the enormous sacrifices made earlier by those who were inadvertently caught up in turmoil. Bosnians can recite from memory the century long periods of peace or war within their national borders, times when Serbian, Croatian, Bosnian and a handful of other successfully or unsuccessfully attempted to make claim and inhabit the same lands.

Bosnian youths are especially aware of their historical roots and nearly all of them have a full understanding about their past. School texts are crammed full with details about times of calm or strife, when Bosnians either lived in peace with their neighbors or clashed with them in horrific battles. All students must successfully pass history in school. But during the war years the nation's history was somewhat altered, newly interpreted by educators who were responding to tensions and believing they were promoting better understanding among their students. Later, the new interpretations proved to be both biased and inaccurate. The educators remained convinced the new interpretations best illustrated current events but later on it became clear that they actually caused confusion, resulting in increased tension between ideologists, historians and students.

To be considered credible, the study of history must be taught entirely accurate. But in the tense atmosphere of war, the new interpretations were often biased in favor of war. Adding to this, many leaders who held power believed that war was inevitable, a situation that could not be avoided. Others even believed war promised increased hope for a better future.

"Most guys my age were pretty straight in their views." Zlatomir said. All of them had benefited by studying from the same school texts during a peaceful and stable time in Bosnia. They had all learned the same lessons and because of this, Zlatomir and the majority of others from his generation shared similar views about their history that were common to the majority of Bosnians. They also shared the same hopes and outlook about their future.

After having enjoyed a good education, they now expected to live in an environment that offered plentiful jobs with good wages and benefits, and a reasonable expectation that peace and security equated a full and satisfying life experience. Once hostilities began however, the average person immediately sensed that full-scale war loomed on the horizon. Most people based their opinions on accounts carried in regional newspapers and periodicals. Everyone engaged in endless streams of gossip about the consideration by those who met up on public streets or in community shops and among families who gathered in the evening around the dinner table. The conversations remained calm until people began to speculate about impending doom.

Then people grew animated from fright and rage.

The average Bosnian was desperately searching for security during a terribly troubling time. People tended to either ignore or overlook any inconsistency voiced by their leaders. They blamed such anomalies on the pressure of the times, the highly charged atmosphere of war. Accuracy was thought to be a luxury few could afford. People were now far more concerned with their own daily survival and that of their families. They clung to information that promised the best hope of avoiding violence and harm. Like people anywhere who face dire threat, Bosnians on the whole adhered to any news that offered the most promise for a secure future.

Still they asked pointed questions of their leaders. Are we facing annihilation? Will blood splatter our front stoop? Will we survive?

In contrast to the heartfelt wishes of the majority of the Bosnian people, certain influential leaders were often convinced of something quite different. Older people, Bosnians with firsthand experience in the horrors of war, knew the terrible price that could be exacted. But certain of their leaders who held enormous power to make decisions remained committed to war because it was the easiest, quickest way to achieve their objective, a war that could determine dominance. There was little room for harmony. Friction best served their objectives. Soon vitriol filled the public forum, speeches, newspaper editorials and additional sources of information aimed at arousing passion and intensifying feelings. The gulf between various segments of the population grew wider.

"They poisoned the way people thought," Zlatomir said of the numerous calls for military action at that time.

Religious leaders jumped into the fray. Pastors, priests and imams, representing the major religions of Bosnia, joined sides. They were no longer in the singular business of spiritual guidance. From behind polished lecterns, they delivered unsettling sermons call for action. Many men of the cloth became convinced war was the only option. Under the guise of preaching the word of God, sermons became veiled calls for war and they helped to sway public opinion to that point of view. Like others, religious leaders were convinced they were on the right path to achieve their mission.

Tensions increased. Educators, a class of people that is respected and admired in Bosnian society, joined their religious colleagues. Educators, capable of molding attitudes among the young, undertook their mission with renewed fervor and zeal. Bosnian teachers are expected to follow standards established by state educators, but many now began to deviate and designed lessons of their own. The new lessons nearly always favored conflict.

Obedient students, conditioned by parents and society to respect authority, rarely objected. They normally devote a great deal of time in committing long tracts of assigned material to memory and classrooms are often conducted in complete silence. Student disobedience is virtually unknown. Interaction between Bosnian students and teachers is minimal at best, and in certain instances, even prohibited.

Many of the teachers in Zlatomir's classrooms were quite old at the time of the war. They had originally been recruited for the job after World War II when countless men and women with a modicum of education were seeking paid employment. An army of new instructors was desperately needed for the numerous classrooms then under construction. Teachers were hired in mass numbers. Many were marginally educated and few held teaching credentials. They were unworldly people, holding narrow provincial views far removed from the mainstream of a modern and progressive society. They were poorly equipped to cope with questions from students who were frequently more sophisticated than them.

The world had grown infinitely smaller by the time this new army of educators arrived. Bosnia was now a much more complex and sophisticated place but many educators, especially those in the rural areas, remained ignorant of change and progress. Bosnia was rapidly emerging as an important voice in Balkan and world affairs, partially brought about by modern communication that significantly increased the flow of vital information. As Bosnia joined the ranks of nations holding international influence, Bosnia's educational system remained stymied and rooted in a dated past by educators who were influenced almost entirely by their own individual environment.

CHAPTER THREE

*I*t started suddenly on the Eid Holiday, April 6, 1992. Chetniks (radi-cal Serbs) and ex-Yugoslav Army regulars from Serbia and Montenegro attacked my hometown, Čapljina, from their strongholds at Gubavica and Pijesci on one side of town, and Stolac on the other side. They had started ethnic cleansing of towns on the Dubrave Plateau.

The unprepared population was not ready to show resistance by or-ganizing because appointed leaders failed to organize and arm them. Those few armed men provided heroic resistance on Mount Bivolje Brdo, but after attacks of Yugo-Army's armored units they had to with-draw to Neretva River. It was hell. Rifles against armored vehicles! People were running from everywhere trying to reach the river. That's where the first victims fell. Two of our fighters lost their life almost at their doorsteps. Rivers of men, women, children and elderly people were coming down to Počitelj from Dubrave Plateau to reach Neretva to reach free territories leaving behind everything they owned and built for generations.

A group of individuals led by Sreten Kapetanović called Kapa, a com-mander of an HVO (Croatian Defense Council) unit in Počitelj built the *plan of how to transfer all of those refugees to the other bank of the river to freedom. Day and night numerous rafts were built to transport people, livestock and cars. And the evacuation began.*

At the time Chetniks and Yugo-Army occupied positions on the left bank in Klepci, Prebilovci, Modrič and Dubrave. At all of these locations local Serbs got organized to conquer territories they recently shared with their Muslim neighbors. They wanted it all for themselves, denying the right to life for Muslims, Croats and Serbs loyal to the idea of multiethnic coexistence, but it was all wishful thinking!

Zlatomir had inadvertently witnessed what the terrorized refugees were fleeing. More than most, he understood what was happening. He sympathized with their plight.

Zlatomir's neighbor Miro Kurtato had asked Zlatomir to drive him to Tasovčići, a neighborhood across the river from Čapljina on the east side of the Neretva. This neighbor, a Bosnian Croat, was married to a Bosnian Serb. Both heritages promised protection in the event they were stopped on the road. The neighbor Miro Kurtato wanted to ensure that his Serb in-laws in Tasovčići were safe but he had no transportation for the trip. Would Zlatomir drive him? On the drive, Zlatomir passed through various hamlets. Things were obviously amiss. Main streets, normally alive with people conducting business or visiting, were deserted, like "ghost towns," according to Zlatomir. Farm animals clamored from pens in vain in need of water and feed and begging for attention. The ground was littered with personal belongings that had been dropped by people during hasty departures, pieces of clothing, odd toys, broken dishes, and scraps of papers, including personal letters from loved ones. Homes were abandoned. Shutters banged in the wind and doors stood ajar, left as they were in a mad race to safety.

Zlatomir met up with his friends in Tosovčići at a local outdoor cafe. "These were people I had known all my life and I wanted to sit and visit with them."

As it turned out, only Bosnian Serbs joined the gathering. Zlatomir was surprised to learn Bosnian Muslims and Bosnian Croats had already fled. What once would have been a full evening of eating and laughter was cut short to a single drink. Zlatomir headed home earlier than normal, knowing it would be some time before he saw these men again. If war came, they would automatically become enemies.

"You cannot be friends with people who are shooting at you. "You cannot be friends with the enemy," Zlatomir explained. "They changed their mind about me too. I became their enemy."

On a short stretch of road home just before the river between Tasovčići and Čapljina, Zlatomir encountered a roadblock manned by guards from the Yugoslavian National Army. He had heard about such roadblocks but this was the first time he had encountered one and been stopped. Bags filled with sand from the nearby riverbank were stacked high and every motorist was halted to a stop by heavily armed guards.

A machine gunner aimed his deadly weapon directly at each car. Zlatomir was neither apprehensive nor nervous. Čapljina is a small settlement and most people know or at least recognize one another from the streets in town or in the outdoor market. As it happened, these were local men and Zlatomir had a nodding relationship with them.

One man, holding a rifle with an ammunition belt strapped to his waist, was a friend of long standing. He whispered a blunt warning of caution. "Leave this area immediately and do not return. Tomorrow we expect Serbian military reinforcements. They will be people we do not know and they will not know us. It will become very dangerous." The afternoon drive, a favor to a neighbor, turned into an unnerving reconnaissance mission. "It was a very dangerous trip," Zlatomir observed in hindsight.

Some 16 months later, the two men recognized one another on the streets in the outdoor market. Zlatomir saw the neighbor Miro

Kurtato who had asked for the favor of a ride and who had done nothing to try and assist at the time of the arrest, which had happened directly next door to the neighbor's house. Zlatomir went hungry for months in the prison camp but Miro Kurtato made no effort to bring food even though it was widely known that prisoners were starving.

Evacuations from Počitelj were mostly executed at night because Chetniks started using artillery fire aiming at the city and surrounding areas. It felt like we were bombarded from all sides around us. From the mount above Počitelj snipers were the busiest ones shooting people in boats. Local Chetniks from Tasovčići were coming to Počitelj to sack and confiscate cars and valuable possessions from frightened refugees and to destroy rafts in order to stop evacuations. At night Chetniks sank rafts and during the day people with help of HVO unit from Počitelj led by its commander Sreten Kapetanović Kapa were building the new ones so that thousands and thousands of lives could be saved.

Simultaneously little pockets of resistance were initiated in Počitelj when all men able to fight were drafted to fight. They had a small still free part of the territory on the left bank from Ševač Njive to Dabrice, a place to prepare and organize where Chetniks didn't dare to come to anymore. To compensate, they were launching artillery fire on the refugees crossing the river in Počitelj to Šurmanci, then down the river in the direction of the town to be evacuated to Croatia.

Most of the men coming form the Dubrave Plateau were redirected to Međugorje to prepare for a counter attack. They were all enlisted in HVO (Croatian Defense Council) and given uniforms and weapons and prepared to go back to the left bank to free Dubrave from occupation.

At the beginning we in apljina self organized, too. With all the happenings in Dubrave where National Guard members from Montenegro and Serbia sacked, robbed and harassed the population, we knew that we would be the next ones as soon as they were done there. Small, scattered groups of armed young men were ready to defend the right banks of the river, the town and the surrounding areas. I enlisted in such a group. There was a long waiting list of people to join but not all could be immediately included because we lacked uniforms and weaponry, however, we all had a strong desire and determination to defend our town, families, dearest ones, friends, neighbors, our homes and our industries. We were ready to sacrifice our lives in order to prevent them from entering our town. Besides Chetniks and Yugo-Army on the left bank we had another enemy behind our backs, the local garrison which is a story on its own. While Chetniks and National Guards were preparing for their attack in Dubrave all of the young regular soldiers were replaced by local members of the National Guard and volunteers. First they evacuated everything they could, all of the Army's equipment and possessions, which were not insignificant. For many days and nights, in front of our eyes, hundreds of trucks were pulling out equipment and weaponry to transport them, as we would later find out, to Serbia. We got orders not to interfere, not do anything on our own initiative to stop the transports.

Local Serb populations started to move out of town and pretty soon only a small number of them were left, those who loved their town and have always enjoyed their lives there. Everything they accomplished and loved was in that town and it didn't make any sense to leave it behind for any reason. Their allegiance and loyalty were to that town. Politics didn't poison their thinking not did they turn them against their neighbors who lived with them side by side, in good and evil, who didn't judge people by the color of their skin or by their beliefs.

Almost all military personnel who lived in town with their families moved out and the rest of them moved into the base in Gabela and Majevica. More than one hundred and twenty trucks of weapons and ammunition were taken away in a short period of time. At the same time they were also taking barrels and barrels of fuel from the national reserve, one of the biggest ones in the ex-Yugoslavia, containing more than eighty million liters of fuel.

They were in a hurry to take away as much as they could, because they knew the day would soon come when they would have to leave Čapljina forever. Simultaneously, they were preparing for the war.

They started harassing the population by firing all kinds of weapons over the city, houses and local factories and shooting women still working despite the circumstances. Some were wounded. We knew then that we would have to conquer the garrison because we could not afford to be "in the sandwich", Chetniks on the left bank, local National Guard on the right and behind our backs. Then the hell broke.

All roads out and in were blocked, we on one side, they on the other and the war cloud above us. The time was up with our very survival in question. We started defining our defense lines by the river. We were digging trenches and building bunkers at night, during the day we were exposed to the constant shelling from the left bank. Plans and preparations for conquering the garrison were ready. Among the chief organizers there were men such as General Praljak, Daidža, Kraljević and Boban. Young specialized forces from HVO and HOS came from Croatia. We were not allowed to participate in the conquest of the base because we were not properly prepared, trained, nor equipped. The base was under siege for many days already. Those inside were called upon to surrender to avoid any victims.

Soon after, around mid April, they used air strikes against us. Military commanders didn't like the idea of their officers being captured, so they sent in planes to bomb us, to create chaos and use choppers to evacuate military men and their families from the base, in which they succeeded but suffered big losses. Two planes were shot down. Choppers were not shot at to avoid retaliation because they could erase Čapljina from the face of the earth. They probably wanted to do that anyway, knowing that the town was lost for them forever and they could never return there ever again, their reasoning being that if they can't have it then no one should. They took us seriously when they lost the planes. With time, a strong air defense was built on our side. In the next few days they lost five more planes above the territories of Čapljina, Metković and Neum. Their attacks were fewer and fewer.

In Čapljina the first local HVO was formed. There were all kinds of Croats military and paramilitary organizations; HV, HVO, HOS, TO. Too many factions were in one place with one common enemy. HVO entered the base and used it for its own purposes. HOS occupied Dretelj and the fuel reserves and kept its units there.

TO found it's base in the "Committee" building near to the town's little mall. I was their member along with Muslims and a few Serbs. The political divisions infiltrated all aspects of our lives and the feeling of everybody going to its own flock started creeping in. HVO's were Croats, TO's were Muslims, HOS's were Croats and Muslims together. Someone had already designed divisions among us. We in TO, were all of the people from downtown. It was easier for us to trust each other knowing that we were raised together, went to school together and shared good and evil together. Here I will mention some of the names so they will not be forgotten. Commander Hamo Dedić, Logistics Sejo Duraković, Džemo Najetović from Zenica an ex Yugo-Army Major. Then brothers Safet and Alija Čolakavić, Nezir Feriz. They were a part of the leadership team, positions earned not by their competencies, but because, so it was said, they had the dough. They helped us get uniforms and weapons. I never understood their roles in our unit. There were rumors that brothers Čolaković by being a part of the unit earned exemptions from paying dues and tariffs at customs while importing goods through Merhamet in Zagreb and Split from abroad. It was well known even then that they owned stores as their private business. Nothing about them was clear and transparent. Time will only tell.

The other members of our unit were Mili Dizdarević, Adem Fazlagić, and others that I grew up with and I have to mention a few; brothers Kurtić, Sejo and Derviš, called Deva, then Troko, Seno Spužić, Bleki, Zule, Seno Bosanac, Eda, Breka, Troko, Dragan, Žane, Đonko, the entire tribe Čolaković (seventeen of them), Avdo Voloder, Ejub Smrda, Eda, Janje, Vajta, Šipto, Roho, Sadat, Žuti, Hogar, Miki, Nane, Baća, Tuca and me, Pirgo, and many others. One hundred of us had uniforms and weapons, the others were on the waiting list. Our responsibility was to protect the areas under the new bridge. We were assigned six-hour shifts. Adjacent to us were members of the "Falcons" unit, led by the legendary Čeprkalo (Martin Bebek). Composed by other friends, Muslims, Croats and a few Serbs left in town, that unit was independent too with their headquarters in the old Post Office building.

The day of the big attack, HOS members were on the other side on day earlier to lead, accompanied with some of our units who took positions around Počitelj. HOS was the first one to get into Klepci, Prebilovci, Tasovčići and they progressed towards Stolac. We followed them. Our unit's route was through Tasovčići, Hotanj, Čučkovina by the river Bregava, Opličići, all the way to Poplate. We were "mopping" terrain and were fortunate not to run into Chetniks. We didn't have to engage in fighting because they were faster to run. For all of that we also have to thank the artillery who also helped clearing our way. Our forces were aiming their positions in a way to leave them a corridor to retreat and to avoid direct fights and victims on either side. The corridor was pointed indirection of Bregava, Hodovo, Sćepan Križ. And that's what happened. They retreated and we took their positions around Stolac, Hodovo, Stanojevići, Trijebanj, Rotimlja, Drenovac and we held them through to the end. However, we the soldiers, are convinced that everything that happened that day was a planned and agreed upon by both the Serb and Croat sides because ever since the line of demarcation did not move an inch. There were shootings and shelling every day, but that was all, no infantry actions. Right next to our positions there were the forces of Army of Bosnia and Hercegovina. They held their positions too, extending the line from Rotimlja to Podveležje. That situation went on for a year, until the escalation of conflicts between HVO and the Bosnian Army in central Bosnia. Little by little those conflicts spread and affected relationships between HVO and Army in our area of responsibility, Mostar. That's how it all began.

Until then I was part of HVO. Our platoon had one hundred and thirty men, Croats and Muslims. One unit had thirty-five men, all Muslims from Tasovčići, with a Croat Sergeant. All leadership was held by Croats. We were not bothered by that because we all had a common enemy, Chetniks from Serbia and Montenegro. The second unit was made up of Croats with a few Serbs from Gabela. The third unit was a majority of Croats, a number *of Muslims and a few Serbs. I was a part of that unit. We were a well-co-ordinated team, however with escalation of conflicts in central Bosnia, the relationships among us changed. Croats in our unit started to empathize and identify with Croats in central Bosnia, accusing Muslims for what was happening there. From one day to the next, they were seeing only what they wanted to see, that is Croats in central Bosnia, "their people", were perse-cuted by Muslims and they "are not doing anything". Up until that time HVO and the Bosnian Army fought together shoulder to shoulder. Their headquarters were in Gubavica and Rotimlja, near to ours. All of our at-tacks, Gradina, Kotašnica and others were always planned and executed together. And then one day in April, HVO units capture and take over the headquarters of the Bosnian Army in Gubavica and Rotimlja. The major-ity of the Army retreated to Blagaj and Mostar. When that happened, not one Muslim was part of it because they were not called to participate. We didn't even know what was happening on the grounds.*

At the same time, persecution against Muslims started in Rotimlja, Buna, Gubavica and Pijesci. All Muslims assigned with a weapon were disarmed with an excuse that weapons were needed on the first lines of de-fense, which eventually turned out to be a lie.

Everything the leadership did was behind our backs, justifying their actions in different ways, hiding the truth. The real truth was they were afraid that one day Muslims would, depending on daily happenings and politics, turn against them.

News of the war exploded onto the world scene in the late af-ternoon of April 6, 1992. Headlines in newspapers around the globe screamed about a cowardly shooting that occurred during a march for peace in Sarajevo, the capital city of the Bosnia and Herzegovina. The city was then the center of a fledgling peace movement where 100,000 Bosnians turned out for the proces-sion, including Bosnians of Croatian and Serbian background, Hungarian and Albanian heritage, and Gypsies and Jews. The crowd surged forward, moving into the old historical district down-town. The front of the crowd had just crossed over the famous

Vrbanja Bridge on the Miljacka River when Serb snipers opened fire from hiding places in the nearby Holiday Inn. Scores on the front were wounded and six were killed, including two young women, Suada Dilberović who was a medical student, and her friend, an ethnic Croat Olga Sučić. The whine of the first bullet turned this peace march into a bloody confrontation that eventually altered the course of European history in the Balkans.

Those participating in the march did not know that earlier in the day Serb paramilitary units had attacked several police stations and a school in the area. The marchers were unprepared for violence and the Serbian sharpshooters caught them entirely by surprise. Shock gave way to horror. People quickly realized their beloved city, a place of peaceful diversity, had instantly become a killing field during a cowardly attack on unarmed civilians. The incident, widely condemned throughout the world, was nearly incomprehensible to the local population. Six snipers were arrested, but were exchanged when the Serbs threatened to kill the commandant of the Bosnian police academy who was captured the previous day, after the Serbs took over the academy and arrested him.

If the intent of the gunmen who murdered Sauda and Olga was to arouse public passion, they succeeded beyond their wildest dreams. The attack was considered an outrage, a violation of civil society. People mourned but their grief was cut short within a day when Serbian troops laid siege on Sarajevo. They pounded the city with heavy artillery guns, causing the residents to run for their lives from screaming bullets and exploding shells. People never imagined then how long the attacks would continue, lasting without pause day after day for nearly four years. In time, the old historic district was reduced to rubble and 15,500 people in the city were killed. When the siege finally ended in 1994, it was the longest attack on a city in the history of modern warfare. Sarajevo, a fabled place of vibrant life, came close to death.

Other lovely and historic Bosnian cities were also destroyed in the same way. The eastern city of Srebrenica was bombed into submission and thousands of men and boys, 8,000 in all, were systematically murdered, ten at a time. Dubrovnik, a Croatian city on the Adriatic Sea, in the region of Dalmatia, one of the most prominent tourist destinations in the Mediterranean Sea, and the center of Dubrovnik-Neretva County was nearly destroyed. Mostar, a city and municipality in southern Bosnia and Herzegovina, the most important city in the Herzegovina region and a short drive from Zlatomir's hometown, was reduced to ruins. Many other small settlements, picturesque villages like Počitelj and Klepci, were entirely destroyed. Others, like Gabela and Dretelj, became dreadful prison camps.

The war also destroyed over one thousand historical sites, including the fabled Old Bridge in Mostar, the century-old city hall and parliament building in downtown Sarajevo, and the great National and University Library of Bosnia-Herzegovina where thousands of rare volumes containing Bosnia's history, were destroyed. The library burned to the ground in a fire started by arsonists. Earlier that year, the archive of the Oriental Institute of Sarajevo, including manuscripts in Bosnian, Turkish, Hebrew, Persian, and Arabic, was obliterated. While Bosnian cities and towns suffered grave destruction, some of the fiercest fighting took place in the countryside. Rural Bosnia was reduced to a littered and ruined place. People living in small, semi-isolated settlements suffered most. They were defenseless, neither armed for war nor trained in combat. Enemy officers labeled these hamlets "easy targets" because they were so easy to invade and capture.

The lovely hills and mountains of rural Bosnia, covered in thick stands of pine and scrub, conspired with the enemy by providing covert hiding places for the enemy who would sneak up on a small, terrified community, enclose it in what they called a "ring of rifles," and then attack with lightning speed. Villages were turned into scenes of death and destruction. Beatings, disfigurement and homicide were the common order of the day.

As fighting grew ever closer to Čapljina, it became evident that it was only a matter of time before hometown and the many small settlements nearby, would be drawn into this infamous ring. Small villages like Počitelj and Dubrave to the north and Klepci and Struge to the south were threatened and were vulnerable.

Montenegro is one of the six new republics to emerge from the ashes of old Yugoslavia. A conservative place, it has always been politically aligned with Serbia. During the war it was only natural that Montenegro would automatically side with Serbia and the country soon became an enemy of Bosnia.

The population was not prepared to resist. Our leaders failed to prepare us. We were not organized or armed. A few men with weapons heroically resisted on Bivolje Brdo but they had to retreat to the Neretva River when the Yugoslavian Army's armored divisions attacked. It was hell, a few rifles against armored vehicles. We in Čapljina then began to organize ourselves. We knew we were the next target.

Čapljina is located three hours southwest of Sarajevo in a municipality of the same name. During the war it was home to some 25,000 people. The town sits at the foot of the vast Dubrave Plateau twelve miles from the Adriatic Sea, in a long temperate valley of fertile fields and orchards, grapevines and olive trees. It is a centrally located Balkan breadbasket and a major transportation center that provides a gateway to the open sea.

Čapljina, dubbed the town on four rivers because it straddles the great river Neretva that is fed by three tributaries, the Trebižat, the Bregava and the Krupa. This scenic beauty on four rivers became hell for its population at the time of war and betrayal in old Yugoslavia. Two bridges, an ancient iron structure named after a former Croatian president Franjo Tuđman, and a modern one of steel, span from bank to bank over the Neretva. The nearby Hutovo Blato provides a vast rich nesting region for 256 species of birds. It is the most diverse avian gathering in Europe and the town is named after one. In English, Čapljina means heron. The heron is clever, standing motionless until prey is spotted and then, with lightning speed, stabbing it with its long, pointed bill.

By early spring in 1992, Čapljina was a town in crisis. A number of things forebode impending violence. Most telling were enormous crowds of refugees flooding through town, headed to the Neretva River and beyond, to Croatia, Hungary, Austria or Italy. While they were not wanted in those places, they hoped to find safety. Their numbers increased daily, thousands of haggard, exhausted people who were hungry, dirty and footsore.

Most Bosnian Muslims were called Bosniaks when the term was included in the new 1993 Bosnian Constitution. Although an ancient term, it was officially included for the census of 1991 so they would have distinction for an accurate census of ethnic background. There were also Bosnians of Croatian and Serbian ancestry that should have been promised protection.

Whatever their heritage, the refuges had been born in Bosnia and had always lived there. They thought of themselves as fully Bosnian.

But these were people who, at great personal risk, refused to support official military aggression then underway. Entire regions in the west where Bosnians of Croatian heritage lived were entirely evacuated. Entire communities of Bosnian Serbs also fled. They moved as one in a terrifying flight for their lives.

CHAPTER FOUR

Major General Lewis MacKenzie, the Canadian commander of the United Nations peacekeeping force in Yugoslavia, was a prominent source of misinformation. He should have known better. His ignorance and consequent actions are said to border on the criminal. Carol Off, a Balkan specialist and author based in Sarajevo, wrote that MacKenzie was willfully ignorant of the Bosnian political situation.

Local rumor had it that MacKenzie enjoyed the pleasure of very young Bosnian women and when photos of his liaisons were made public, his tenure was cut short little more than a year later. MacKenzie's most egregious error was in portraying Bosnians as killers of Bosnians, a tactic that he said was meant to generate international sympathy and attention. "Both sides are shelling themselves," he reported. He was later criticized for a "lack of judgment" by UN officials after receiving money from SerbNet, a Serbian-American lobbyist group, adding fuel to rumors that MacKenzie privately favored Serbia in the war.

At first, Croatian president Franjo Tuđman supported Bosnians in their effort to defend against Serbian attacks. Huge numbers of men from Herzegovina in southern Bosnia enlisted in the Croatian Army, including Zlatomir and his closest lifelong friends. They were convinced the Croats were their best bet in defending their hometowns that lay close to the Croatian border. The Croatian army had just emerged successfully from a short-lived, violent war with the Serbs that lasted six months, from the summer of 1991 to January 1992. It was even reported that Croatian troops received four days leave whenever they delivered a pair of enemy ears to commanding officers.

Zlatomir detailed Bosnia's Croat allies in his journal.

The important role of Croatian paramilitary forces cannot be forgotten, men and women who took the lead after already seeing combat in Vukovar, Brod and other places.

They were courageous, disciplined and well prepared, real role models. They caused havoc by sabotaging the Chetniks, crossing the river and entering enemy positions. We were amazed. The Chetniks were terrified of them and their black uniforms. Their commander was Sajo. Nobody knew his real name, and his lieutenant was Miro Hrstić.

By summer of 1993, Tuđman changed course and he turned on the Croat army in Bosnia after he and Alija Izetbegović, Bosnia's president, secretly plotted to split the country evenly between them. Such a move was unpopular in many places, including the United States. When Tuđman attended the opening of the Holocaust National Museum in Washington, DC in 1993, he was loudly booed. Tuđman, a staunch supporter of Germany during World War II who died of cancer in office, was never able to implement one of his more onerous ideas, renaming city streets after former infamous Ustashe terrorists during World War II. Recall of the murderous Ustashe remains a vivid scar among older Bosnians who witnessed the mayhem and violence by the group that looted and murdered with abandon. Few Ustashe were ever brought to justice for their unspeakable crimes. Many Bosnians who had lost loved ones to them lived with this devastating reality.

Tuđman's about turn on Bosnia had far reaching impact on men like Zlatomir who unwittingly fell victim to one of the most cunning betrayals in modern warfare. Without warning or advanced knowledge, Bosnian militias were incorporated into the Croatian army through a deal cut by Bosnian president Alija Izetbegović and Tuđman. Izetbegović had little choice but to bow to Croat demands. He was in no position to face down such a powerful enemy.

Men like Zlatomir, Bosnian by birth and residency, were instantly suspect. He and others like him had fought alongside Croatian troops and proved loyal to the Croat-Bosnia alliance. But place of birth assumed more importance and this lone fact would eventually prove fatal to those born Bosnian. They were arrested without recourse and sent to concentration camps in southern Bosnia.

The destiny of the war between Serbia and Croatia was actually set from the beginning by Milošević and Tuđman during semi-secret talks between the two in March 1991. Yugoslavian names held little significance by militias from each country. Newly cleaned areas of majority Croat would become Croatian and new areas of majority Serb would become Serbian. Once cleaned, no region in Bosnia would be seen as multiethnic.

CHAPTER FIVE

Zlatomir was caught up in the web of war for the most elementary of reasons, like the names of the men in his family. Other than during brief periods of heightened prejudices during earlier world wars, Yugoslavian names carried little significance until the Bosnian War. The family name was Šarić (Sharich) when the family lived in Yugoslavia. An older brother, who became a U.S. naturalized citizen years later, changed the spelling to Saric. He wanted to make the name easier to pronounce and spell in English. Whether Saric or Šarić (Sharich), family members maintain the interchangeable name that is "international," meaning it does not signify either ethnic or religious heritage.

The trouble for the Šarić family came from the first name of the elder Šarić. Šerif. It is a familiar Muslim name. The Šarić family considered his first name a minor detail, not worthy of thinking about. They never attempted to keep the name private or to hide it. Adding to this, Šerif's second eldest son, a noted academic in Sarajevo, was given a Muslim name, Taib. Now, two members in the family carried decidedly Muslim names.

Later, when Zlatomir was stopped in downtown Čapljina on his way to the town's base, the policeman was asked his father's name at a roadblock in downtown Čapljina. Zlatomir did not hesitate in saying Šerif. The family was in the minority.

The river Neretva also innocently played into the scheme hatched by Milošević and Tuđman. Bosnia is a lush land criss-crossed by numerous waterways and lakes. A prominent waterway is the Neretva, flowing south from mountains in the north until emptying many miles later into the Adriatic Sea.

Over the centuries, the river has created a natural boundary. Towns located west of the river are primarily populated by ethnic Croats and those to the east are predominately ethnic Serb. This settlement pattern proved useful to invading troops bent on div-vying up the country between Croatia and Serbia. Entire ethnic regions were dispersed on nothing more than this.

Three main communities, Mostar to the north, Metković to the south and Čapljina, which is situated between the two, are nearly equal distance from one another. Directly across the river from Čapljina is the settlement of Počitelj and below are the small towns of Mogorjelo, Struge and Gabela, site of the infamous prison camp. The scenic Hutovo Blato hills are north, near the town of Klepci. Stolac is a few miles west of Čapljina.

By 1991, the Yugoslavian National Army was a huge, popular force of 600,000 men. Formerly called the Yugoslavian People's Army National, it first organized during World War II in the small Bosnian town of Rudo. 'Day of the Army' and 'Victory Day' cel-ebrations are staged annually in every community with complete orchestra music in village squares, marching bands and parades in the streets and dancing at night. The army is meant to "defend borders against aggressors," and delay invasion long enough for local militia to step up. By the late 1980's, this charge underwent a deadly change. Bosnian Serbs secretly restructured officer and enlistment corps and turned the military into a force dominated by Serbs. In May1992, the army was renamed the Military for the Federal Republic of Yugoslavia. The name was a misnomer. The army was no longer meant to serve all Yugoslavians.

Bosnia's population is intrinsically similar to that of any country that welcomes immigrant communities. Immigrants normally join populations that are already established and homogenous within the larger community. Newcomers settle in and become part of the local landscape, solidifying their position through citizenship. Arabs from Africa are now French citizens. Turks are now German citizens. Vietnamese are Australian. Zlatomir is now American.

The ancestry of the Šarić family is a snapshot of a typical Bosnian family. In the far background there is a hint of Croatian blood but it is so far removed that details have long been forgotten. Both Šarić parents were decidedly Bosnian of long standing. His father grew up in Čeljevo, a small village just outside Čapljina and his mother was raised in Čapljina. Both were atheists, typical of the times, they neither practiced religion nor passed it along to their children. To support his family Zlatomir's father operated a small business, purchasing eel from local fishermen, smoking the eel and exporting it to Austria and Germany. During World War II, the family lost everything and had to start anew. His father became a salesman in town. The couple was married 40 years when Zlatomirs's father unexpectedly died of a heart attack in the 1975. His mother died 29 years later in the United States at age 94. She was living with her elderly sister in an apartment in Seattle, near her three sons and their families. The elderly sister, Zlatomir's aunt returned to Bosnia and continues to live in the old family home in Čapljina.

Bosnians are a mosaic of different nationalities, a veritable ethnic kaleidoscope that forms the core of the country. They share common ethics that weave a cohesive population. Above all,

Bosnians are loyal to family and friends. They are always polite and civil, and they're protective of themselves and others. This has been so for as long as anyone can remember.

Bosniaks and Bosnians of Croat and Serbian heritage constitute the majority of the populations, living alongside Bosnians of Hungarian and Albanian backgrounds, Roma or gypsies and Jews who make up the smallest communities.

Bosnians take such differences easily in stride, paying little attention to what for them is perfectly natural and normal. Tolerance is considered an admirable trait, a national ethic that runs deep.

It stretches the imagination to think a murderous conflict could conceivably begin over differences between people who had lived together as neighbors for unknown generations, stretching back hundreds of years. Such reasoning flies in the face of hard facts. Yet it remained the primary reason provided by political pundits for years.

Marshal Josip Broz knew as well as any about diversity and his foresight on the subject would prove to be frighteningly prescient. Better known by his nickname 'Tito,' which translates "do it," Josip Broz was born to a Slovene mother and a Croat father. Tito led Yugoslavia from 1946 until his death in 1980, harnessing the nation's diversity and forging it into a strong elixir. Tito's glue was a simple slogan, "Unity and Brotherhood." Regardless of nationality, all citizens are equal. The concept began early on, taught in the earliest grades at school and reinforced by conscientious parents. It contributed to an overall sense of harmony in all spheres of society. Tito reassured people that by suppressing nationalism, the future was infinitely brighter and more promising than it had been in previous generations.

Tito, a charismatic former World War II partisan, is considered the chief architect of the Second Yugoslavia or "Titoism." Wielding stern leadership, Tito introduced innovative policies that led to prosperity. He stood up to powerful leaders in the Soviet Union and the United States and they took him seriously when he boasted he could mobilize eight million troops in 24 hours. During his forty years as a leader, Tito opened Yugoslavia to the world, growing into a respected and adept statesman along the way.

Under Titoism, religion took a decidedly back seat in society. Bosnia has not been a spiritual nation since the introduction of Communism after World War II. By 1990 multiple generations of Bosnians had grown into adulthood nearly devoid of religious rites. Most modern citizens considered the subject an anachronism, parochial traditions that had little role in a progressive modern society. The elderly, those reared on a conservative diet of religion, continued to worship but attendance at religious services remained small.

Atheism in the Šarić family extends back multiple generations, mainly due to Communists rule when religion and faith were eschewed. Catholicism played no role in the family ethics. It was neither practiced in the home nor paid any heed. Most people at that time professed to being either atheist or agnostic. People outside the family who did not know them well mistakenly thought the Šarićs might be Muslim, primarily for a single reason. The elder Šarić's first name was Šerif, a name of decidedly Muslim origin. When his second son was born, Šerif gave the baby a name that is also entirely of Muslim origin, Taib. With two members of the family carrying Muslim first names, it is understandable that those who did not know better thought they were Muslim. The majority of the population in Bosnia is Muslim so the conclusion would not seem out of the ordinary. The Šarićs were unconcerned about the notion and did nothing to dispel it.

Ethnicity, like religion, also grew increasingly irrelevant as a means of identification in the new Yugoslavia. It was an unpopular concept no longer in favor and only ever considered by a very few. During interviews, Zlatomir was even taken aback when asked to identify the ethnicity of his closest friends he had known his entire life. He was caught by surprise. He had never before been asked something like this. He thought a moment but he was unable to fully describe the ethnicity of these close friends.

"Nobody knew who was Serb, Croat or Muslim," Zlatomir said. Furthermore, "nobody cared."

Based on census reports in early 1991, a time when the threat of war hung heavily in the air, scores of people considered themselves "Yugoslavian " and they called themselves Yugoslavian. The majority effectively eliminated personal forms of identity such as ethnicity and religion. Even after the country imploded and the country of Yugoslavia no longer existed, the trend continued. It was no loner a viable form of identification because the country was gone but people continue to think of themselves as Yugoslavian. Yugoslav is their nationality. But with war upon them, people slowly began to change their response and began to identify themselves by the republic where they resided. At the height of the war in 1992, some eleven percent of people living in Bosnia identified themselves to be Bosnian.

Members of the Šarić family continue to call themselves Yugoslavian, both those still living in Bosnia and those who have settled abroad. Every member of the family agreed to this designation long ago and each remains steadfast with the original decision. It is, they believe, a means of remaining fair and neutral with all Yugoslavians, especially during a terrible time when the country splintered into separate republics. They have been pressured by others from the old country to update their nationality from Yugoslavian to Bosnian. But the Šarićs remain comfortable with their original decision. Nobody in the family has ever considered changing their national identity and it is unlikely anyone will ever do so. Zlatomir thinks of himself as Yugoslavian American.

We were pushed to take a side, to name ourselves after our republic of Bosnia. But, we decided not to. We took a stand on this. Not many other people did it like us. People fought over this issue and attacked those who didn't agree with them. So, we had to be careful and protect ourselves.

Until 1991 there was no category for Muslims. During the national census that year, a constitutional change created a new category, Bosniak. It is now the designated nationality for Slavic Muslims who, once counted, outnumbered Bosnian Croats and Serbs. Two additional groups, Jews and Roma, are forbidden by the Bosnian constitution to seek the presidency but constitutionality of the issue is currently under consideration by the European Court of Human Rights. Ironically, five hundred years before, Bosnia was the first European nation to welcome Jews. During the 20th century, they grew into ethnic targets and fewer than 1,000 live in the Bosnia today.

Like ethnicity, the Šarić family's religious identification is also thought by many to be Islam. They lived in a country that is majority Muslim and the eldest male in the family carried a Muslim name, Šerif. A second son, now a respected academic in Sarejevo, was also given a Muslim name, Taib. The family's religious root was Catholic but religion played no role and had not for many generations. The family lived in a country with which the majority were Muslim and were never practicing Catholics. There was nothing to counter the erroneous Muslim label. Heritage and ethnicity has never been an issue in the family and has never accounted for animosity between the siblings or their mates. Most Bosnians at this time were either atheist or agnostic. But later on, religion would play a significant role in the lives of several family members.

Mixed marriages illustrate the lack of interest in ethnic identification. Between 1981 and 1991, twenty percent of all marriages were between people of different ethnic backgrounds.

Zlatomir's family is telling. Bosnian by birth and residency, Zlatomir and an older sister who died young were the only two to marry Bosnians. Three brothers and a sister married Bosnian Croats and a remaining brother married a Bosnian Serb. Such designations refer only to family background that is often from the distant past. Only the eldest sister married non-Bosnian, a man from Serbia that she met when he was temporarily employed in her hometown. By 1990 ethnic divisions had largely disappeared in the cities and intermarriage, according to author Christopher Bennett, was so common that in Sarajevo it was almost impossible to find someone without relatives from a different ethnic background.

Conversely, when loyalties were stretched thin and tested beyond endurance during and following the Bosnia war, mixed marriage was cited as the primary cause for divorce. As pressures on identity increased, it impacted people who previously had paid it no attention. Zlatomir and his wife of 13 years divorced shortly before the hostilities began. Their divorce was the result of issues totally unrelated to the war. One of the few photographs Zlatomir has from the past was taken immediately after the wedding ceremony. A tall beaming groom dressed in a dark suit with a full head of dark, curly hair stands beside a diminutive bride who appears to be quite young and seems to be quite terrified. She became a bride in the old way. Zlatomir's closest friends, men who know he was quite taken with the young woman, picked her up from her house in the small Čapljina suburb where she lived and carried her to Zlatomir. Under mores of the time, neither Zlatomir nor the young woman could disavow the act. Marriage was the only option. Until the mid-19th century, many Bosnian marriages were arranged in this manner.

As expected, Bosnian men of fighting age lined up for war according to ethnic heritage and family bias, casually passed along as it is in all families from one generation to the next. Except during brief periods in World War I and World War II, heritage had nearly always remained a benign subject registering little importance. Now however, for the first time in memory it began assuming greater importance. Bosnian sons of Croat and Serbian heritage began to prepare for war. Many were roused into action by ugly propaganda campaigns aimed at Bosniaks.

CHAPTER SIX

As expected, Bosnian men of fighting age lined up for war according to ethnic heritage and family bias, casually passed along as it is in all families from one generation to the next. Except during brief periods in World Wars I and II, heritage had nearly always remained a benign subject registering little importance. Now, however, for the first time in memory it began assuming greater importance. Bosnian sons of Croat and Serbian heritage began to prepare for war. Many were roused into action by ugly propaganda campaigns aimed at Bosniaks. Few of these young enlistees knew much about either Serbia or Croatia, only what they had learned in school. They had never visited either country. Now they were willing to shed their blood in defense of their country.

Once war erupted, Zlatomir faced few options other than enlisting in the military. All men between sixteen and sixty years of age were expected to serve and eventually every man did. By volunteering for service, Zlatomir was able to select where he wanted to serve in Bosnia. He opted for the Čapljina area. Otherwise, he was certain to be drafted, which meant he could face assignment anywhere in the country where he was most needed. In April 1992, he joined the Patriots Liga.

The young men shared mutual confusion. They had come of age under Tito's slogan of 'brotherhood,' believing they were brothers with one another in ancestry and nationality. Yet, the country was now divided into seven separate republics. Were they still brothers? Did shared ancestry and nationality still count? It was a conundrum for all.

More important issues took precedence over history and heritage. The first order of the day was to remain safe and alive.

The threat of war weighed heavily, especially uncertainties over the timing and nature of attacks. In Čapljina, people could clearly hear the echo of exploding shells and bombs in the historical city of Dubrovnik some 100 miles east. As the attack grew in intensity, floods of refugees once again increased in size after having slowed in recent weeks. Streams of people again poured through town, lugging their pitiful belongings and carrying children too young to walk. They were a constant reminder of ethnic cleansing.

Serbian snipers, well hidden in the hills continued their murderous fire, aiming at pedestrians on the roadways below. But their job had grown more challenging. People quickly grew accustomed to gunfire. The sound of the first shot sent pedestrians dodging, running and hiding, often in basements of the nearest available building, or dropping flat onto the street and quickly ducking for cover behind a parked car, a tree not yet chopped down for firewood, a trash barrel, or even the curb running alongside the street. Anything that offered even the slightest protection was used. More often than not, the quick evasive action meant sharpshooters increasingly failed to hit potential victims.

Dragan Mračević was among Zlatomir's closest friends. He was wounded twice, once when crossing the airport landing strip when he was hit by enemy gunfire. The second shooting was different. He was shot in the back during a firefight with Serbian troops.

The bullet hit a protective vest Dragan was wearing at the time but if it had hit an inch higher, he would likely have been killed. Dragan knew he was wounded by someone in his fighting unit but he never knew exactly who. It could have been any one of the fifty or so men in his unit. They were from nearby towns and villages and they some took umbrage at Dragan's heritage. His father was Montenegrin, the republic most supportive of the Serbian invasion.

Montenegrin troops, known as fierce fighters, had participated in some of the most vicious attacks on Bosnians, provoking mindless terror and horrible atrocities. After he was shot, Dragan confided in Zlatomir: "You never know who is going to shoot you or when."

Serbian roadblocks effectively cut off contact from Čapljina to the outside world. Phones were useless. Lines were downed or had been cut by the enemy. Cell phones were unknown. Trails over the mountains, filled with loose gravel and rocks, were difficult to traverse and required hours of hiking. Bridges that connected the west side of the Neretva River to the east, both the new modern bridge and the old iron one, had been repeatedly bombed and were now ruined fragments submerged in the river below. Locals were happy to see the destruction of the new bridge because it had been named after Franjo Tuđman.

The rivers and lakes of Bosnia were useful places for invading troops to dispose of corpses that multiplied in large numbers. Countless bodies were thrown into various waterways from city bridges, like the one in Višegrad. So many bodies lodged in sections of the Drina River that the manager of the local hydroelectric plant appealed to all concerned for a stop to this practice. Bodies were lodging in various sections of the Drina River. An occasional corpse floated down the river.

Čapljinans tried their best to maintain normal lives. When bombardments landed in the town, emergency crews were immediately dispatched to clean up rubble on the roads. The job was danger-ous and poorly paid but men were grateful for the work.

Many families were barely eking out a minimum existence. When the hostilities started many jobs suddenly ceased to exist and hours were severely cut on employment that continued. The only available new employment work was tied to the war effort, either manufacturing armaments or joining the military. Otherwise, there was virtually nothing else to do. In time, people in need be-gan selling family treasures and heirlooms for whatever price the traffic would bear.

People burned furniture for warmth and once that source of fuel was gone, wooden floor planks were pried up and burned. Then small stands of trees some distance from town began disap-pearing. Trees were chopped down without mercy for use as fuel. For the elderly who had lived through the last world war, this was déjà vu of hard times and survival was the order of the day.

Small militias began to organize in neighborhoods throughout Čapljina. Zlatomir and his four closest friends were still living in the Bombardeli apartment building near downtown where they had grown up together. Žane, Dragan, Troko, Tuca and Zlatomir who was always called by his nickname Pirgo. The word means freckle in the language of Bosnia. His parents had settled into the apartment years before and once at home. Bosnians normally stay put, and rarely move elsewhere.

Neighbors commonly grow quite close and it is not uncommon for neighbors to refer to one another as relatives. The Šarić apart-ment continues to be occupied by a family member, an elderly aunt, and nobody in the family would ever consider selling it.

The five men were tight as boys, running in a pack to explore both the town and the nearby countryside. The Neretva River, lo-cated a short distance from the apartment building, was a favorite haunt, especially a small island in the middle of the river.

Abandoned donkeys and miniature horses lived on the island. The boys risked bites and kicks, climbing atop the animals. On occasions, they even rode an animal home where they were confronted by parents who were aghast and ordered the animals be immediately returned to the island. Zlatomir still carries a faint scar on one calf in the shape of a burro's mouth.

As teens, the five disappeared for a night or days at a time. They ignored directives by their parents if they threatened to interfere with new adventure. They savoured all things unknown and forbidden, and were especially happy when their adrenalin peaked. They spent nights with foreign girls who were backpacking through the picturesque countryside near the homes of the teens. One summer they hitched rides to Italy where they slept in caves with a myriad of young women. They were confident and strutted with swagger, pushing limits as far as possible, but not so far as to ever court legal trouble.

Bombardeli was one of a row of identical high-rise apartment buildings on a broad avenue next to town, a block from the powerful Neretva. The local school was just down the street, the police department around the corner. Only civilian families lived in the Bombardeli. Apartment buildings on either side of the street with different names were filled with military families. But now few were left. Most had already fled town under the threat of war.

Zlatomir was living with his elderly widowed mother. He had evacuated her from Čapljina to a sister's home in Croatia. But when the threat of fighting in town quieted, he responded to his mother's pleas. She wanted to return to her home so Zlatomir brought her back to the apartment.

He still marvels that not a single resident of Bombardeli, people of every ethnicity, turned against one another during the days leading up to war.

We knew our town was next and we were ready to sacrifice our lives to prevent the enemy from entering it.

All of us were prepared to fight in defence of our loved ones and our friends, our homes and our industry.

All young men able to fight were drafted and began to organize. I enlisted in a fighting group. Not everyone who enlisted could be immediately accommodated because we lacked uniforms and weapons. Small, scattered groups were armed. The first pockets of resistance started in a small free area on the east bank of the Neretva near Počitelj, between the villages of Ševač Njive and Dabrice. Chetniks dared not enter the free area.

The time was up and our very survival was in question. We started defining our defence line by the river. At night we dug trenches and built bunkers. During the day we were exposed to the constant shelling.

Once organized, the Bombardeli men and others in their unit were in desperate need of weapons and ammunition. Their arsenal was scarce. They only had a few ancient rifles from World War II and some old family pistols. Then someone remembered military training classes at the local school. The classroom was raided and the rifles and ammunition they found were quickly scooped up. But the ammunition proved to be a problem. It was not live. To prevent unfortunate accidents at school, students only practiced marksmanship with blank cartridges. The blanks sounded like live bullets but carried no punch and offered no protection. Still, everyone reasoned that in the heat of battle, the enemy could never differentiate between the sound of a blank and real the thing. So the ammunition was also taken.

One very cold and quiet morning we were on the front line of the River Neretva, Žane, Dragan, Troko, Tuca, Deva and I. Through the crisp air I heard my little buddy, Sejo Kurtić call me in a whisper. "Pirgo, Pirgo. Come here you guys, I made coffee." Using a coca cola can, he had dug a hole in the hard cold ground to make the coffee so no smoke from the little fire could be seen. Even though we were tired and cold we all left our heavy coats and guns behind us in the bunker and eagerly crawled on our bellies fifty to sixty meters to our friend for the hot coffee. As soon as we got to Sejo and the inviting hot liquid we heard a grenade coming towards us. This scared us since this had never happened before during the war. The loud noise of the grenade exploding on our bunker made us forget about the *coffee. Amazed that we were all still alive, shivering from fight and cold, we cautiously waited about ten minutes in case the Serbs sent another grenade before we crawled back to our bunker. The bunker, our coats and guns were shredded all over with grenade shrapnel.*

We were lucky that day. We owe this miracle to Sejo and his coffee. He saved our lives. Troko, Dragan, Tuca and I tried to find out where this grenade came from over many years when we would reminisce about the war and the miracle of how we survived this explosion. To this day we puzzle over the mystery of what possessed Sejo to make coffee and call us to him this one early morning. Whatever created this series of events certainly saved our lives and we are forever grateful to our friend and his coffee.

The shortage of weapons remained critical to the Bosnians throughout the war. It was a crucial problem known by everyone, even the enemy. Bosnian troops were out-armed and out-gunned the entire war. Whenever friendly combatants managed to sneak through Serb lines into town, they ferried as many extra weapons as possible. But this was merely a stopgap measure, resulting in few extra weapons. Meanwhile, the desperate search continued.

By this time most Bosnian military personnel of Serbian heritage and their families living in town had already left Čapljina. Few noticed when they began slipping away leaving everything behind in the mistaken belief they would soon return and reclaim their goods and homes. Those who stayed behind moved into the safety of a small military installation west of town simply referred to as the fort. Within days, helicopters commanded by Serb pilots landed at the fort and spirited everyone there away, flying east towards Serbia. Airplanes accompanied the helicopters, providing diversion by bombing the town during the evacuation of Bosnian Serbs.

Serb commanders did not want their officers captured so air strikes began in mid-April. Serb military and families were evacuated but at great loss. Two planes were shot down. We built a strong air defence and in the next few days they lost five more planes above the towns Čapljina, Metković and Neum. They began to take us seriously.

We did not shoot at the choppers because we knew they could erase Čapljina from the face of the earth. They probably wanted to do that anyway because the town was lost to them. They knew they could not return. They probably reasoned that if they could not have the town, nobody should have it.

The fort was now the focus of attention. Years before, the site of the fort had been carefully selected by military leaders because of its' strategic location. The site was nearly equal distance between Serbia and Croatia. The fort was a holding facility for munitions and fuel, and one hundred trucks were parked at the site.

Once the facility fell into Serbian control, enemy drivers hauled away tons of munitions and the largest reserve of fuel in Yugoslavia, some 80 million litres/gallons from a nearby military base in Gabela, Majevica. The job was finished as quickly as possible for fear of retaliation by local Bosnian troops.

For days and nights, right in front of our eyes, we watched them pulling out equipment, weaponry and oil. People in town later learned munitions that had been stored in Čapljina for decades, were transported to Serbia and then used to attack the very citizens who, for many years, had served as caretakers of it all.

CHAPTER SEVEN

An incident in early spring focused full attention on the fort. A neighbor Zlatomir had known for years was shot and killed when he visited the fort's small infirmary for a daily injection of insulin for a diabetic condition. Dragan Bajramović was a well-liked man from a respected family who had retired from a career in the Yugoslavian army. Dragan's father had for years served as the town's elected representative to Bosnia's national parliament. On this day Dragan drove to the dispensary as usual. But things had changed since his last visit the day before. Guards of long standing known to everyone in town had been replaced with a set of strangers, young Serbian troops who were not familiar with Čapljinans. Later, the story spread that Dragan had lectured the young men about what he believed to be their misguided intentions. The conversation escalated and turned ugly. In the heat of the moment a young guard drew his pistol and shot him dead. Bajramović was unarmed. People never imagined such a stunning incident would ever happen in their quiet town.

Following the incident, Bosniak and Croat conscripts deserted their posts, leaving behind only soldiers of Serbian background. Without a shot being fired, the fort fell entirely into Serbian hands.

While many people of Serb ancestry who had taken refuge at the fort were flown out of town, many others chose to stay in Čapljina. They willingly faced the unknown at home rather than flee. Some among them were briefly imprisoned in camps a mile from town in the small villages of Dretelj and Gabela, but once Croat troops took control of the area, they were immediately released.

They loved their town and their loyalty was here. They saw no reason to leave. It didn't make sense to them. They didn't let politics poison their thinking. They didn't turn against their neighbors.

In large part they were unable to help their beleaguered Muslim neighbors. There simply were too few of them to make any real difference and virtually none of them were armed. But local Bosnian Serbs did fulfill one vital role in the beginning. It is widely believed the town was spared earlier attacks and bombing because Serbian troops and pilots were reluctant to fire on ethnic cousins they knew to still be living in and around town.

During the WWII, the Croatian Ustashe regime did massacre in the village of Prebilovci. The population was nearly exterminated. Some six hundred people, half the population, were thrown into deep pits. Those who did not die immediately were shot. Fifty-seven families were exterminated and it was nearly three decades later before the first young man from the village was old enough for military duty in the Yugoslav army.

The Bosnian War was the second time in the Twentieth Century that this Balkan region became a battlefield. During World War II, Croat nationalists in Bosnia known as the Ustashe attacked Serb nationalists called Chetniks. Thousands were murdered and millions forced from their homes. In an ironic twist, positions had turned in this most recent war. They were the exact opposite.

Croats, previously the aggressors, were now the hunted. In this latest war, Bosnian Serbs attacked Bosnian Croats, fueled by rage and hated that were based on stories from the past by memories of the elderly. In both wars, neighbor attacked neighbor. Those living for generations in the region, passing houses along to upcoming generations and who expected to remain neighbors far into the future, became instant enemies. It was a form of self-preservation. And in both wars, innocent women, children and pensioners were the primary victims, caught up in violence of war and paying the ultimate price.

Facing an army of Bosnia Serbs from the east and a second line of attack from the Serb-controlled fort, Čapljina was in a vulnerable "sandwich." The men of Bombardeli prepared for war. Armed with an array of old guns and blank cartridges, with many dressed in street clothes and tennis shoes, they joined others in much the same poor condition. Each unit was independent from the other, coordinated by leaders of the Patriot League. One unit from Tasovčići consisted of thirty-five Muslims led by a Croat. Another consisted of men with Croat and Serb heritage all from the village of Gabela. Zlatomir's unit had one hundred and thirty men, a mix of Bosniaks or Muslims and Bosnian Croats. Croatian and Bosnian fighters were, according to Zlatomir, "*a well coordinated team, fighting together, shoulder to shoulder. All our attacks were always planned and executed together.*"

Headquarters for both Croatian and Bosnian armies were located side by side in the towns of Gubavica and Rotimlja. Every unit shared an enormous charge: protect Čapljina from marauding Serb fighters who had already proven what they were capable of in other small communities that had already been decimated.

One hundred of us had uniforms and weapons. The others were on the waiting list. Our responsibility was to protect the area under the new bridge, preventing the enemy from crossing over. We were assigned to twelve-hour shifts. Adjacent to us were member of "Falcons" unit, led by legendary Martin Bebek, called Čeprkalo. Composed by other friends, Muslims, Croats and few Serbs left in town, our unit was independent, too with headquarters in the old post office building.

The lack of weapons was a major problem and all means possible were considered to increase the Bosnian arsenal.

Throughout the war the Bosnians remained under-armed. Croat fighters snuck into town and always ferried extra rifles that were passed along to others. Occasionally someone would show up with a single rifle for sale, probably stolen elsewhere. Other times an entire truck shipment of weapons would disappear and then turn up for sale later by the thieves.

Weapons were purchased on a thriving black market run by local criminals who made enormous profits selling whatever they could get their hands on, either legally or not. Significant numbers of weapons finally arrived from Croatia, crates packed full and ferried into town in huge trucks. The crates of armaments were distributed at "gun bazaars" held in local community centers and from the garages of private homes. Fighters wandered about selecting weapons of choice from boxes or from tables heavily laden with a variety of guns and other weapons. Zlatomir opted for a machine gun because it reminded him of the 1920s gangster Al Capone. He named it "Meka Čuna," domestic slang that he says has no translation. For the next year the weapon rarely left his side.

Still, a chronic shortage of weapons remained. Only those who could afford it actually purchased a weapon and carried it at all times. There were always more fighters than there were weapons to arm them. When men went on patrol, those who were unarmed, barrowed pistols and rifles from comrades who stayed behind. The same was true of uniforms. Many men from the Čapljina area often went to war dressed in jeans and tennis shoes.

Zlatomir had served in the Yugoslav Army immediately after high school graduation, from 1973 to 1974. Because Zlatomir enlisted earlier and was an experienced militiaman he was signed in to Zlatomir's outfit.

Fighters from around the world stepped forward to assist the beleaguered Bosnians, especially from countries in the Middle East. Men identified with the Bosnians because of what they perceived to be a shared Muslim heritage. No matter that most Bosnians were not religious, cared little about religion and knew virtually nothing about the Islamic faith. Countries in the Middle East were interested in converts and the pragmatic Bosnians were happy to accept help from any quarter. They simply allowed misimpressions to stand.

Hearing of the possible riches to be had in the war Balkan criminals plying their schemes in Europe and elsewhere flocked back to Bosnia. They wanted a fair share of whatever riches might become available. Balkan fugitives hiding from the law throughout Europe, America and Australia also returned home. Criminals and fugitives joined existing paramilitary groups or formed their own. They closely guarded their actual identities by using such nicknames as Ćelo, Juka and Caca. Few others, including Zlatomir, ever learned their actual identities.

Illegal enterprises during the war were frequently successful and often conducted on the battlefield. Bribes ensured government officials and military leaders to turn a blind eye to such things.

Balkan men serving in the Foreign Legion also returned to Bosnia, deserting the Legion and ready for war at home. Their actual identities were also a closely guarded secret by Legionnaire leaders because many were fugitive from the law and living elsewhere under assumed names.

Criminal paramilitary groups in Sarajevo also cashed in. Notorious criminals each controlled their own territories.

The start of the war in Bosnia and Hercegovina is officially set as April 6, 1992 the day the two young women marching for peace in Sarajevo were shot and killed by Serb snipers. But people in southern Bosnia Hercegovina knew hostilities had started months earlier, in January 1992. Then Serbs moved heavy artillery into the mountains and hills east of Čapljina, the Žegulja and Hrgud mountains north and south of the nearby town of Stolac. Artillery was also moved into the village of Prebilovci, an all-Serb community southeast of Čapljina.

Everyone in Čapljina felt certain this was the precursor of war, but people continued to hold on to the hope, that the appearance of such armaments, were intended only to intimidate the local populace. They persisted in the belief that an agreement between the two sides would eventually result in a resolution without bloodshed.

"We thought that the country would be split without shooting and that everybody would be happy with the solution because we had no choice. Take everything you must, but just don't kill. This thinking was a big mistake," Zlatomir realized early on.

Although Čapljina was spared actual warfare on the streets of town, nearby hamlets were easily invaded and captured. Places like Stolac, a village southeast of Čapljina, was invaded by from either side. Terrified people abandoned homes in advance of enemy troops, fleeing the threat of war and leaving behind everything of value. They left in such a hurry that hapless dogs remained tied to fence posts and farm animals were left in pens and corrals without food or water.

By this time, villages in the Dubrave Plateau below the mountains east of Čapljina were already ethnically cleaned. Then bombing began, with rockets and mortar shells lobbed by heavy artillery from the hilltops into the valley below where Čapljina lay vulnerable. People scrambled to avoid harm, seeking safety wherever possible, primarily in the surrounding islands of pine trees. Still, Serbian armies captured many folks in town and held them prisoner.

Once Serbs were airlifted from the fort in town, hostilities quieted, providing enough time for mop-up operations. Later Zlatomir's unit was ordered door to door on the heels of the Serb invasion. They searched for weapons and gasoline that remained hidden and had been inadvertently overlooked during original searches by the enemy.

What they found instead were disturbing scenes of daily life that were obviously rudely interrupted by the arrival of the invading enemy troops. Towns were deserted.

Only the elderly, who had been unable to flee on foot, were left behind terrified and vulnerable. Some cooking stoves that were heated by wood remained warm to the touch. Women had been in the process of preparing family meals when forced to flee. Tables in other homes were set for meals, complete with untouched food wafting delicious aromas.

The troops were hungry, surviving for days and weeks on meager rations of unappetizing cold food straight from tin cans.

As much as they wanted, nobody ate a single bite of anything. It could possibly be poisoned. Worse, the table might be rigged to explode from the slightest pressure, like picking up a piece of bread or moving a dish. In the basement of one house huge vats of homemade wine were discovered alongside a handmade still. No matter how tempting, nobody drank a drop. The wine could be poisoned. Instead, troops used the wine to wash feet that were in much need of a good cleaning because running water was scarce. In one yard, men stared at a multitude of ripe cherries hanging from a tree in full bloom. Although starving, they avoided the tempting fruit. Instead, they placed flags around the perimeter, warning others about the possibility of buried mines at the base of the tree.

Vitriolic messages on the airwaves continued to amp up animosities between people where there had previously been nothing more than occasional normal animus. At first, people ignored the vitriol. But among those who continued listening, the messages eventually began to take hold, slowly at first but more quickly in time. Inspired by lies heard over the radio or seen on TV, people grew motivated to take up arms and fight to the death.

Bosnians were ignorant of the meetings between Milošević and Tuđman. Only later would they learn that the two leaders were in constant phone contact. During twenty-eight phone calls between the two, they plotted to destroy Bosnia and divide the country between them. Throughout the war the men on the ground knew nothing about either the phone calls or the secret plots. They remained ignorant of such traitorous acts until such information was made public following the end of the war. Milošević and Tuđman were tried in The Hague and both received lengthy prison sentences for their nefarious deeds.

On the first Sunday in June, was "Cherry Sunday" in Počitelj, Bosnian fighters on the west side of the Neretva River gained an edge over Serbian fighters on the east bank of the river. Using rafts, small boats and even wading across, the Bosnians forcing them back some twenty miles behind what had once been their front line. Now the Bosnians had a new and second front line that was further from home. The Bosnian gain was significant. It even seemed possible to route the enemy. But they had received strict orders from headquarters that they were not to advance any further than the first front line which was adjacent to the Neretva on the east side. This was an order that was repeatedly carried out by military leaders.

General Blaž Kraljević stretched the order and used their own cars to move munitions from place to place or to transport munitions captured from the Serbs.

During one battle, Croatian and Bosnian troops faced off against the Serbians. Militia from opposite sides of a small canyon covered in pine just outside the ancient settlement of Stolac in southern Hercegovina. During peacetime Stolac is a haven for intellectuals and artisans and the region is a popular hunting ground, teeming with deer and other wild animals that range among trees and prehistoric ruins. Zlatomir's unit was caught at one end on the west side of the canyon. It was essential that weapons and ammunition be transferred to the opposite end. It meant crossing from one stand of pine to the other, over an ancient mile-wide Roman road covered in macadam. During the crossing each driver would become a tempting target, a sitting duck during the time it took to traverse the area. Serbian gunners firing mortars and rockets from Howitzers on the opposite bank of the canyon were close enough to be accurate.

Tanks, bombed into submission anti-aircraft guns, mortars, bazookas, rifles and MAC 10 machine guns sliced through air, creating a gut wrenching noise.

To pick the driver, everyone agreed to a simple plan.

Whoever pulled the shortest string from a bundle of thread would drive. Strings were drawn. Zlatomir drew the shortest. He was the designated driver. The only good news was the only available vehicle in the area was his own car and he was familiar with how it handled. Before starting the drive, Zlatomir turned and elicited a promise from Dragan.

I sat in my car and I knew I had to get to the other side. There was no other way to go except forward. I told my good friend Dragan that if I died in this action I wanted 'Monia' (a popular French tune) played at my funeral. It was my wish and he promised.

After I crossed and got to a safe place, I realized how lucky I was. Only then was I scared. My god! This was war and staying alive meant always being alert. You needed to have your eyes open all the time because we are always trying to go a little bit forward and they are also trying to go a little bit forward.

From the journal, written in late 1993 before secret negotiations to partition Bosnia by Tuđman and Milošević were made public:

We, the soldiers, were convinced everything that happened that day was planned and agreed upon between the Serb and Croat sides because once the line of demarcation was established, it never moved an inch. There were shootings and shelling every day, but no infantry action. Right next to our positions were forces from the Bosnia-Hercegovina army. They held their positions, extending the line of defense from Rotimlja to Podveležje. This situation maintained for a year, until the escalation of conflicts between the Croat Defense Council (HVO) and the Bosnian Army in central Bosnia. Little by little those conflicts spread, affecting relationships in our area where we were responsible for Mostar. That's how it all began.

There is normally little humor during the throes of war. It is usually viewed by the sane as an exercise in insanity. Still, there can be light moments. During World War II bears and storks once wandered the streets of Belgrade in Serbia after German bombing raids broke apart cages in the local zoo. The animals, probably confused yet delighted by their newfound freedom, roamed city streets until smelling the water of the Danube where they finally dispersed into nearby fields and forests where their offspring likely continue to reside.

Zlatomir detailed another incident in his journal that could be construed as somewhat humorous at the time.

We *were in position by the river under the bridge when we heard singing by the Chetniks who were burning Muslim and Croat homes in Tasovčići.*

They were drinking and shooting guns into the air. We had heard about these paramilitary units, the White Eagles and the Šešeljevci. They had come from Serbia to help Bosnian Serbs.

Both the White Eagles or Avengers as they were also known, and the Šešeljevci were volunteer units, part of the hard-line Serbian movement that espoused strong, right wing nationalist ideas that allowed for no compromise. They are blamed for the most brutal atrocities of ethnic cleansing during the war. The White Eagles were organized by Mirko Jović under the national Serbian symbol of the double-headed white eagle with a crown and was made up of both men and women. He envisioned an Orthodox Serbia without any Muslims whom Jović considered "nonbelievers."

The Šešeljevci were led by Vojislav Šešelj, an academic who once taught in the United States. He is now on trial for war crimes in The Hague.

To get even, a fighter named Nane went to town and came back with a megaphone, a tape recorder and tapes of Ustashe songs. We called out by name the local Chetniks we knew were there in the enemy lines.

The front lines for both Bosnians and Serbs were set on either side of the river, close enough to clearly see and recognize one another through field glasses. The Bosnians saw men they knew or recognized from town, former classmates and old friends. Now they were the enemy. Everyone on both sides were nervous and bored. They were also in a sour mood and intended to antagonize one another. Men from both sides of the conflict shouted across the river, calling each other vulgar names and yelling out obscenities that are uniquely Bosnian.

Our shouts were perfectly audible in the quiet of night, easily reaching across the river. When we called out to someone by name, they would respond with a rain of fire. Then we started playing national Bosnian songs on the tape recorder and they went ballistic with incessant firing.

We had to crawl deeper into our trenches and bunkers. We couldn't even stick our noses out because of firing from the other side. People from town came running to help. They thought the Chetniks were trying to cross the river.

The unit I was in was great. We did a number of things like this. We were jolly fellows, all for one and one for all. And we knew how to use weapons. We had two 60 mm mortars, two machine guns, two RPG and a few Zolje. None of us had died yet, although a hotel by the bridge and several houses and apartments were hit directly with mortars and burned to the ground.

CHAPTER EIGHT

That night when Zlatomir returned home from a long day of fighting on the front lines, a neighbor named Brna invited Zlatomir and Miro Muminagić to join him for a drink of cognac. Although Brna and Zlatomir had been neighbors for thirty years, this was the first time they had ever met socially to visit. Brna, a town clerk, lived in the unit directly above Zlatomir, and had watched Zlatomir grow into an adult. He had also known Zlatomir's father who had died eighteen years earlier of heart failure. Zlatomir's mother was again home in Čapljina after a brief sojourn in the safety of a daughter's home in Croatia.

Zlatomir, Miro Muminagić and Brna sat on the patio in front of the apartment building, drinking and quietly chatting about events of the moment. Zlatomir vividly recalls the evening because it was so unusual that the two were socializing. Zlatomir had lived next to Brna his entire life and they were close in age. Yet, this was the first time he had been invited for a drink. Later, Zlatomir realized that Brna probably initiated the visit because he was aware of mass arrests scheduled for the following day.

The Bosnian Croat military in town had been ordered to arrest all of Čapljina's Bosniaks on July 1. At first, anyone with a Muslim name was harassed and then arrested. Brna did not warn Zlatomir of the impending action, nor did any other local Croat sound a warning. These were people Zlatomir had known his entire life. He remains convinced to this day that every Bosnian of Croat descent in Čapljina knew about the impending arrests.

The evening ended and Zlatomir retired home where he was living with his mother. Zlatomir was so certain war would not come to his hometown that after driving his mother to a sister's house in Croatia, he made a return trip in response to her pleas to return home. The old woman, then in her late 80s, preferred being in the community where she had many friends and neighbors of long standing. The home was a source of many strong memories, the place where she had raised her family and experienced the earlier deaths of her husband and an adult daughter. Since there seemed no real reason to permanently evacuate her, her youngest son brought her back to Čapljina. Neither realized this evening's visit would be their last for some time.

Čapljina lies in a valley at the bottom of a mountain range, on the west side of the Neretva River. This became the front lines of battle. The Bosnians and their allies held the west side of the river, the Serbs the east side where in January 1992 they installed big guns, tanks and cannons in the hills and mountains above Čapljina. For several months, people conducted daily routines under the constant threat of fire that often missed the intended mark. The assaults were short lived. Once they ended, people emerged from basements and other hiding places, and continued on with daily life. In time, the attacks almost felt normal, certainly nothing uncommon and not nearly as threatening as in the beginning. The residents of Čapljina had little choice. They had to eek out survival amid threatening terror and they did so. Zlatomir said: "They stayed over our heads. They shot over our heads. But we tried to live normal lives."

Employees gave up trying to get to work, realizing they were risking their lives on the streets. The availability of goods and services grew ever more scarce.

By now schools were closed for good. Children lucky enough to live in neighborhoods still filled with other children, met in small groups and continued studying in private homes taught by parents and others. Bosnians perhaps appreciate the value of education more than many others. During World War II their educational system faltered and nearly collapsed when many schoolhouses were burned to the ground and teachers were summarily shot and killed. Fewer than one thousand schools and three thousand educators assumed responsibility for an entire population of students. Since then, education had always assumed great importance.

Accommodations were also made for "our most precious little citizens," some thirty-five thousand children who were wounded in the war, either physically injured or emotionally traumatized. Another sixteen thousand were killed or are permanently missing. Many of the children are believed to be buried in unmarked graves, but the locations remain unknown. Children are especially vulnerable during any war, especially if parents die or vanish and there is no adult able to step into the breach. Most abandoned children were so-called 'rape babies,' born of mothers who suffered assaults by the enemy and had become pregnant. Mothers were often too traumatized to care for their infants. Others found themselves repulsed by the sight of the baby. In the years since the war government authorities in Bosnia and Croatia have refused to register these babies or to recognize women who have been raped as victims of war.

The attacks renewed in earnest during early April. After months of minor skirmishes by Serbian troops "living over our heads," artillery and mortar rounds rained down from the hills and mountains. Serb forces dug in at the village of Prebilovci, a small town whose entire population was of Serbian heritage. This latest round of fire was aimed at Čapljina and Mostar, a five hundred year old city just north of Čapljina. This time the intensity of the attacks did not abate. War had finally arrived in full force. Zlatomir said, "We knew it was time to go to war for good."

Fighting had begun in Southern Bosnia, spreading from Croatia, where Serbs had attacked months earlier. It gradually moved northward until it entered Bosnia.

At one point during the fighting, Bosnian troops crossed over the Neretva, either wading across shallow parts of the river near Počitelj or crossing over on makeshift rafts. They silently stole up the hills towards the higher mountains. As darkness arrived, troops dug in, falling into exhausted sleep in sleeping bags on the ground. No weapons were fired. "We needed to be very quiet so as to not alert the enemy." We chased Serbs 20 miles east and that became the new front lines.

Đonko, a huge man from Čapljina was in Zlatomir's unit. He was known to be an undue braggart. He claimed that war did not unsettle him. In fact, everyone knew he startled at every sound. One dark night Đonko heard a distant noise and, fearing the enemy might be creeping near, he fired a single shot into the inky blackness. The next day troops discovered the small body of a popular gray donkey, dead from a single bullet wound. The donkey had been a popular attraction in the fabled tourist town of Počitelj where families delighted in taking photos of their children atop the much-loved animal who had a pleasant, docile disposition. Now, like so much else in this war, he was gone from local lore, totally erased by death.

Men in the unit often experienced idle time in between battles. One day, they "barrowed" a cow form a nearby field and sprayed her with water. They told Đonko the cow had swum the Neretva and had been led to the local butchery where she was being carved into two- pound packages of meat, free of charge to anyone for the asking. Đonko raced to the butchery for his fair share, only to learn the entire story was a ruse, a teasing way to ease tension during trying times.

Help for the overwhelmed Bosnians came from a variety of sources. Caritas, a Catholic charity sponsored by the Vatican, and Merhamet, a Turkish humanitarian organization, provided shipments of food and other necessities to both civilians and militia. They also provided professional advice to government officials on a variety of issues that carried economic and political importance.

By this time few families had cash left on hand and what money they did have was of little or no value. But it was not a critical problem because there was so little to purchase. People parted with what items of value they still owned, selling them at any price. Then they began to rely on aid agencies for relief.

Big war started in Dubrovnik, Croats attacking, moved into Bosnia. One day started shooting every week. Serbia and Montenegro "never came on foot", never invaded Čapljina, but bombed town.

As the war crept ever closer to Čapljina, moving north from Croatia in the south, small villages began to fall. Enemy troops raped, murdered and stole, and set fires that sometimes burned entire communities to the ground. Following the Serb attacks, Zlatomir's unit was among those ordered out on cleanup operations. During these operations, they discovered hastily written accounts by locals who had suffered under the bombardments and wanted to record the atrocities before fleeing for safety.

This war was really about stealing, stealing anything and everything that could be stolen. Enemy military drivers arrived in huge trucks that were hastily loaded up with munitions and electronic equipment from military warehouses under control of the enemy. The moment a rig was fully loaded, drivers raced back to Sarajevo to sell the goods on the black market

*operating in the underground. Areas without enough weapons or ammu-
nition to conduct war grew vulnerable. Vukovar, for example was such a
town. It was wiped out during an attack. Abandoned homes were ransacked for valuables and yards were excavated in hunts for buried jewelry
and other treasures. Anything discovered of value was taken and later sold
to the highest bidder.*

Hearing of the riches that appeared to be possible and desperately wanting to share in the largess, Bosnian criminals who
had earlier escaped justice at home by fleeing to areas throughout Europe, flocked back home. Criminals arrived in Bosnia and
joined existing paramilitary groups or organized their own units.
The criminals found success in their pursuit of stolen goods and
other valuable items. They were easy to obtain because government officials who were often bribed provided a green light to
steal by turning a blind eye.

Among those who arrived in Bosnia were Mudjahedin from the
Middle East and Africa. They believed they were supporting their
bothers by entering the fracas. They formed the Seventh Muslim
Mountain Brigade called the El Mudjahedin unit, under the leadership of Rasim Delić. As early as 1991, many men in the unit ap-
plied for Bosnia citizenship. It was a natural enough move.

Bosnia is noted as the most multi-ethnic and multi-religious
republic in the former Yugoslavia. Following the war some
Mudjahedins stayed in the country. They married Bosnian wom-
en, purchased homes and settled into jobs, primarily in the town
of Maglaj in central Bosnia. But since 2006 Bosnian hospital-
ity has substantially altered. Over six hundred of those who originally stayed, were forced by Bosnian authorities to return to their
countries of origin. They left for Turkey, Egypt, Syria and Algeria.
Bosnian courts have ruled that these men have no rights with which
to challenge legal proceedings.

Criminal paramilitary groups from Sarajevo, each operating in
their own territory within the city, included such leaders as Ćelo,

Juka and Caca. Their real identities have never been uncovered because, according to Zlatomir, "men closed their mouths" when speaking with authorities. But immediately following the end of hostilities many of these former leaders died under mysterious circumstances, either in unexplained accidents or unusual ways. "If men told, many names would come out,"

Zlatomir speculates.

Zlatomir felt the criminal units provided assistance that was both "good and bad." According to him they helped by slowing down or even stopping the advance of Serbian troops and tanks into Sarajevo and other communities, saving them from total destruction. They helped fight in a vicious war for nearly four years. They obtained essential arms for Bosnian troops from the huge military industrial center in Vogošća. But Zlatomir also said they created certain problems because they only fought by their own rules. They ignored orders from military leaders, never answering to authority. He described them as "very independent" and that trait sometimes caused sticky problems.

Mladen Naletić, familiarly known as Tuta, was a prominent criminal who led a notorious paramilitary unit called the Convicts' Battalion. Tuta was a Bosnian of Croat heritage who managed a casino in Australia before returning to Bosnia for the war. The Battalion was strongly linked to organized crime in Zagreb where Naletić received his orders. Naletić quickly teamed up with the secret police whose ranks were filled with Communists of mainly Bosnian Serb background. Tuta, a murderer and torturer, is best known for using Muslims as human shields in battle. Muslim men were forced onto the front lines of battle, providing protection for those behind them.

Tuta recruited men for his Battalion from local jails, freeing men who were being held on a variety of criminal charges. He promised them freedom and protection from future arrest. In exchange, the former prisoners willingly risked injury or even possible death in battle. Most felt it a fair exchange, preferring the risk of death to languishing in jail. They eagerly signed up for the duty. Men accustomed to breaking the law were now officially sanctioned to continue doing so under the banner of war. They could rape or rob free from the worry of arrest. Crooked officials had been paid to turn a blind eye and to ignore what was happening right before them.

"They were given a green light," Zlatomir said. It had since been documented that ninety percent of all crimes committed during the war were the result of criminals returning to Bosnia and committing new crimes.

We fight alongside the criminals. We are together against the enemy. I don't care if I am fighting alongside a criminal. In that moment we are on the same side. So, I don't complain. Bullets can strike you, no matter who you are next to. The government covered the dirty job, of recruiting criminals, meaning the government actually bribed criminals into active military service.

For one period of several weeks, Zlatomir fought alongside Čeprkalo. Zlatomir and Čeprkalo fought alongside one another until one evening Čeprkalo simply vanished. He slipped away in the dark of night. When Zlatomir next heard of Čeprkalo, he was leading his own paramilitary unit of fighters.

The use of criminals in the military was a 'secret' that every fighter knew. Stories were passed along from one man to the next, both rumors and factual accounts based on firsthand knowledge by witnesses. Deals were made either in secret or out in the open, even occurring on the front lines of battle. A tank, for example, would be driven to the frontlines of battle. Enemy leaders would meet and barter over the price of the vehicle. Once a deal was made, the weapon of war was sold to the enemy. It could likely be used later against those who participated in the deal. It mattered little if it was sold to the enemy. The enormous amounts of money involved in such transactions reduced or eliminated any sense of harm. A tank, for example, could fetch up to ten thousand dollars. This sum made such dangerous deals worthwhile.

Another lucrative source that promised additional income was collecting items left on the battlefield by dead men. Once a battle ended, there were certain men who would scour the scene, searching for items of value from the bodies of the dead. They collected personal items like eyeglasses or pocketknives that had been dropped in death. These items were also sold to the highest bidder.

To pump up his forces, Milošević recruited criminals from Serbia and other regions of the world. Most were men who had earlier left Yugoslavia to escape legal charges for prior offences.

They were now residents in other countries and some even obtained citizenship in adopted homelands. They were drawn back to Yugoslavia by a set of enticing promises, personal riches and a major fight. There were few requirements to participate, although previous experience in an actual battle was considered a bonus. These recruits were able and willing to fight with a mindless fury. Criminals from as far away as the United States, Europe, Australia and elsewhere, joined up. After the war, many of them who stayed in country died in surprisingly high numbers, usually in odd accidents or other mysterious tragedies that seemed to follow foreigners who had fought in Yugoslavia.

The United Nations likes to come to Bosnia because this is Europe. Bosnia has a very educated, high-thinking population, we are not like Africa.

It was also widely known by the majority of Bosnians that throughout the war the black market was primarily operated by the 'blue helmets." They were peace keepers provided by the United Nations, military officers and soldiers, civilian police officers and other personnel who were readily identified by the blue helmets they wore. In a lengthy report by the U.S. AID Office of Foreign Disaster Assistance, a whopping one hundred sixty-five billion dollars were contributed by donor nations to build a sustainable peace in Bosnia. It was the most money ever spent by the U.N. in an industrialized country with a solid middle-class population.

The blue helmets had easy access in and out of Bosnia, allowing them freedom to import and sell goods at will. It is rumored that they earned enormous profits from this illegal trade. "They sold everything and everyone knew it. They made big money," Zlatomir said, adding that they even sold their own packaged food, replacing it with food that was locally available. Blue helmets would hijack entire trucks carrying valuable loads of weapons and ammunition, and sell them to the highest bidder. This resulted in shortages of munitions in places where the trucks were intended to be unloaded, leaving soldiers in dangerous situations.

During the war, prostitution also grew increasingly common. Desperate teen girls and boys could earn money enough in one evening to feed an entire family. "A coerced child would lay down with the enemy because they needed to eat," Zlatomir said. Youth without parents or any other adult to protect them were especially vulnerable,

Sexual violence, especially rape, was so common that it grew into a credible war tactic, employed as an effective weapon of war. Bosnia/Balkan children automatically inherit ethnicity from their father so Serbian militia knew that women who became pregnant by them would bear future Serbians. Rapes were commonly committed in front of family members, military personnel and others. Teen boys were also victims of sexual violence but there is little documentation or information available about this. Following the war, women who had been raped commonly encountered their rapists on the streets of town, in the markets and on the roadways. Many rapists were never brought to justice for their crimes.

CHAPTER NINE

*J*uly 1*st*, *I got up earlier than usual, put on my uniform and went to check in at the headquarters, responding to a non-scheduled call for duty from the night before. (The regular calls would usually come for already scheduled shifts). At the train station I was stopped by the police and they asked for my ID. I gave them my pass. The policeman flipped the pass back and forth several times and asked for my father's name. When I told him 'Šerif', one of the guards got into the passenger side of my car with his machine gun aimed at my stomach and ordered me to drive to the police station. Not knowing what this was all about, and thinking this must have been some mistake, I started up my car, and we soon arrived at the police station. They ordered me to park the car and to go inside to check in. Not suspecting anything, I did everything they told me. When I got inside the police station, a policeman told me to go to the second floor. In one of the offices, I handed over my keys, driver's license and registration to my yellow Zastava 101 Fiat car, to officer Vinko Proleta. I was forced to sign the papers releasing my car for the "needs of civil protection". Still not suspecting anything, I was taken to the first floor where they took me to a larger office. I found there several men, all Muslims who went through the same thing as I did.*

We waited there and soon more young men were brought in. Nobody knew what was waiting for us outside.

They ordered us to follow them outside to a waiting black police car that was idling, then they crammed us in like the worst criminals. Ten of us in such a small space, without windows or any fresh air. The day was very hot. We were still incredulous, still believing all of this was just some kind of a mistake, as they drove us to Dretelj, a small village a mile or so from the town of Čapljina where the Barracks were located.

Years later, on his first return visit home, Zlatomir learned the car was still in town, driven daily on the streets of Čapljina by a man Zlatomir had previously knew. When he first heard this news, Zlatomir let loose with a string of colorful obscenities unique to Balkan men.

Originally a Yugoslav National Army barracks, the camp consisted of six tin warehouses or hangers and two concrete ammunition storage tunnels dug into the hillside where reserve fuel was once stored. Dretelj was part of a vast network of prisons and concentration camps operated and maintained throughout the war by Croatian forces. Thousands of Bosniaks were detained under inhumane conditions in the barracks, deprived of basic necessities like water. Prisoners suffered terrible treatment, including physical and psychological abuse, beatings and sexual assaults.

Unknown to the majority of the captured soldiers, Croatian forces had the year before detained Serb civilians in the camp under equally horrible conditions. Without consideration of civilian or military status, women, the elderly, and children were imprisoned, including boys younger than sixteen years and men over sixty years.

Zlatomir arrived in Dretelj on July 1, 1993, when the prison population was the highest. It was an especially frenzied time, when scores of men were apprehended simply because of their Bosnian heritage. They were identified by family name and arrested by comrades who only days before had been in the same military units. Men were snatched off the streets of town or from nearby battlefields. Although people of both Croatian and Bosnian heritage had lived peacefully as neighbors for as long as anyone in this generation could remember, they had now become bitter enemies divided by religion, politics and above all, revenge.

"The HVO (Croatian Defense Council) arrested everyone they believed didn't think like them. But we were all Bosnian," Zlatomir said in an effort to explain the confusing situation. It is complex because of the many mixed nationalities that live in Bosnia and who fought in the war. Intermarriage between people of Bosnian, Serbian and Croatian heritage was common. Nobody in Zlatomir's generation had ever paid it more than a passing thought.

Some 2,300 Bosniak men were detained during that summer, a time when temperatures were unseasonably hot, spiking upwards to one hundred degrees for weeks on end. Such heat is most unusual in the Balkans.

We arrived at police headquarters in Dretelj. Out front there were several policemen who ordered us to line up and empty our pockets. When I turned around I saw about twenty empty backpacks with contents scattered all around the place. This was the moment when I knew something was very wrong. Something big was happening. After our passes and identification were confiscated, they led us to one of the hangers where there were about 100 men being held. It was 9 a.m..

I felt lost but when I looked around I saw that I knew most of the men. They were all locals from Čapljina. I learned from them that they too, were arrested either that morning or the night before and then brought to Dretelj. Why? Nobody knew and nobody could figure it out.

In early July, Croat forces conducted mass arrests throughout Čapljina and the surrounding area for two weeks. Those who were arrested were understandably confused. Only a short time before, the men who were arresting them had been military colleagues. They had fought alongside one another and now they were being detained with little or no explanation. The only common thread between the arrested men is they were all Bosniaks. Before it was over, every man believed to be Muslim and serving in the Croatian army was eventually arrested. No effort was made to identify military detainees from civilians, or to provide for the release of civilian detainees who had inadvertently been arrested. Of those that were eventually released, many were deported by the Croatian authorities, to other countries. The irony was that Zlatomir was not Muslim.

A number of younger troops were brought in directly from the front lines. From one moment to the next, new groups arrived and more men were put in the hangers. Around noon they brought in my brother Miro (Pop). Throughout the day they were bringing in more and more people, putting them in the hangers and the two tunnels. Eventually there were five hundred of us in two hundred and fifty square meters.

It was horrible, heat, anxiety, sweat and thirst. There was no place to sit. The place was filthy, filled with cement dust. We tried to organize, looking for pieces of wood or boards to sit on. The number of men continued to increase throughout the day.

They began bringing in people that were unknown to us so we concluded that they were not just arresting men in Čapljina but from all around the area. Around noon they brought in my brother Miro. I knew they would pick him up."

When arrested, Miro (Pop) had been playing backgammon at a café in town with an older brother who was not arrested possibly because of his advanced age. Another old man, a Muslim, playing the game with the brothers also escaped arrest, probably for the same reason.

Of the five close friends that enlisted together in the Croatian Army, men who as carefree boys grew into adults caught up in a catastrophic war, all were eventually arrested and detained in various prison camps. "We couldn't escape. We were too well known in town and they kept their eyes on us, Zlatomir said.

Žane evaded arrest the longest by hiding in the forest on the small island of Ada in the Neretva River near Čapljina. He eventually traded his freedom for that of his teen son after authorities arrested the boy. Troko and Dragan were in the mountains near Sarajevo where they had gone to fight with the Bosnian army. Dragan, who made many attempts to rescue a much younger sister in Serbia, was wounded twice, shot once in the arm when driving across the airport runway and a second time in the back by military colleagues, probably because of his ancestry. Only one of the original five, Troko, ended up in the Dretelj prison with Zlatomir.

Another old friend named Zlatko, a local radio announcer, was also in Dretelj when Zlatomir arrived. He was quite sick. Fortunately, medication was available. A plethora of varying pills were traded among the prisoners, pills of every hue and shape. Nobody knew for certain what the pills were meant to cure, but armed with little other than instinct, prisoners relied on the medications to help those in need, the sick and the injured. Every prisoner, whether sick or not, downed the pills in hopes of warding off infection and illness while mired in such unsanitary conditions. Zlatomir obtained a variety of pills and fed them to his sick friend. Zlatko eventually rallied from his illness and after the war, immigrated to Holland.

None of the guards were talking to us in the prison camp. They just kept bringing in more people, sometimes directly from the front lines. Some were unknown to us so we concluded that it was not just men from Čapljina who were being arrested, but men from all around the area. More prisoners were brought in throughout that night. We didn't know how many there were or where they were coming from.

The heat was unbearable and prisoners suffered from both thirst and hunger. The first night, prisoners broke every window in the barracks when men began panicking for air. In response, prison camp guards randomly fired at the building, threatening to shoot the next person who broke a window.

In the summer of 1993, temperatures in Hercegovina were unseasonably hot. Spring and summer had arrived early enough, forcing nearby winter sport arenas to close early. The region normally enjoys a moderate Mediterranean clime, with short winters of snow and mild summers. But during July and August of this year, thermometers spiked higher than normal, with temperatures in the high 90 degrees for weeks at a time. Bosnians were not accustomed to such intense heat and it greatly added to their misery.

Nobody slept that first night or for many nights thereafter. Moans and cries pierced the air, echoing throughout the hanger. Some men panicked in the dark unknown and others were suffering with wounds from savage beatings. All the men spent long hours lying on the hanger's concrete floors. The cement was numbing, sending up chills through clothing and the thin blankets that had been distributed. Outside temperatures never seemed to impact the cement. It never warmed. A short board, one-inch thick offered relief to the lucky person temporarily in possession of it. The chill was unable to penetrate the board. The board was passed around, shared by everyone at one time or another.

By morning, prisoners had not received food or water since their arrest the day before. They begged for water but guards would only give water to prisoners who had a container. Zlatomir and his friends eventually found two plastic bottles that each contained 1.5 litres. The supply was better than nothing at all, but the small amount was not nearly enough for the many in need.

We would fill the bottle cap with water and pass it to each person, just enough to wet our lips. The remainder of the water was distributed to young teen boys and old men locked in with us.

Around noon a truck stopped in front of each of the three hangers, unloading heaps of old Yugoslavian army uniforms.

Prisoners in HVO uniforms were ordered to change into any uniform lying on the ground. We were told that we were imprisoned indefinitely "for our own safety. A great reason for so many arrests!"

On the second day in camp the prisoners received their daily meal late in the afternoon. It was meagre, a small bowl of gruel with a spoon and a small chunk of bread. There was no choice but to eat it. Men were already passing out from hunger. Starvation eventually became a chronic condition that left prisoners susceptible to infectious diseases that, without treatment, could rapidly turn deadly.

Miro and I settled down in the middle of the hanger, as far away as possible from doors and windows, seeking safety by disappearing in the crowd. We were in Hanger 2-D. All around us were folks from downtown: Adem Fazlagić, Zlatko Alajbegović, Ataf, Kuga and his sons Asim and Diho, Galama, Fazla, Firstik, Kečo, Lule, Žika Pačonja, Caka, Zlatan Hasanagić, Šicko, Rajko, Brzac, Biza, Naser, Eno Mrga, Šipto, Tuca, Eso, Haso, Aziz, Živac, Musair and his son Haris, Bato, Idriz, Kema, Baluba, Kiko Rumonja, Faruk, Emir Mrgan, Huso Feriz, Ado, Mara, Muta, Suljo Kuhar, Štronci, Senad Bosanac, Naćo, Medo, Nijaz Šaldo, and many others from Stolac, Dubrave i Prozor.

Torture had already started, physical and psychological mistreatment, so we knew we would not be released anytime soon. The guards did not want civilians outside the camp to learn about what was happening inside.

The people outside continually rushed the wire fencing that surrounded the camp. They were relatives and friends who carried plastic bags filled with food meant for loved ones inside, cakes, bread and jam, coffee and sugar. But few of the goods actually reached the prisoners. The guards stole the food and either ate it or sold it on the black market. Medicines also intended for the detainees were also stolen and sold by the guards.

Among those milling around outside were volunteers from the United Nations and other similar agencies based in both Arabia and Europe, including France, Italy and Germany. They were pressing to force the closure of the camp in Dretelj. To some degree they succeeded. In early 1993, a few prisoners from the Dretelj prison were reportedly released. But it was little more than a public show for the volunteer monitors. The detainees in Dretelj were transferred to a second prison camp at Gabela, located several miles away in the small town of Gabela.

United Nations monitors and others assisted war victims in other vital ways, especially Germany, a country held in high esteem by many Bosnians today. Some three hundred fifty thousand Bosnian refugees found sanctuary in Germany on trains that ran non-stop from Čapljina to Germany.

The guards started making lists of our names. People from Red Cross arrived inside camp and also made lists, identifying people who were in mixed marriages with Croats, and those who had sisters married to Croats. They told us these people would be freed first. We had false hopes that this was true, that we would be freed because of Croatian connections.

Days passed, one after the other, a monotony of agony that included suffocating heat during the day, severe thirst and hunger, and long nights on the frigid concrete. The men were not allowed to move, forced to relieve themselves in the same place where they slept.

We urinated in plastic bottles and then emptied them through the windows.

Some prisoners were forced to drink their own urine to survive. We defecated in plastic bags and threw them out the windows. The wind blew the stench back in. There were millions of flies but, surprisingly, no mosquitoes that year. Actually, they were probably better off somewhere else because it was so horrible in the camp.

We volunteered for work groups that left camp each day for manual labour outside. Every prisoner agreed it was much better labouring outside than staying inside with little or nothing to occupy our time. There was also the faint hope that once outside, a prisoner might encounter or recognize somebody, a soldier, a policeman, or a civilian not yet poisoned by ideas of nationalism that had invaded so many among the populace in such a negative way. Perhaps they might be willing to help the prisoners by passing along a message to families, or some generous soul might offer a slice of bread or a cigarette. Most important, being outside increased the possibility of hearing news about the war and reaction to it beyond Bosnia.

Much of our information came in this way so we knew a lot of what was happening outside. But we also ended up with a lot of misinformation.

Work groups spent most of each day outside the prison. Lucky men worked at jobs they had performed in peacetime. Mechanics, for example, worked in improvised garages, repairing and upgrading vehicles now used by the police. They included a wide range of automobiles that had been confiscated from owners at the time of arrest. Zlatomir's Fiat was undoubtedly part of this fleet.

Other work groups, like the one Zlatomir most often worked with, were assigned to the front lines where they spent long dangerous days digging trenches and building bunkers for their captors. The prisoners feared being shot by their own troops who were some distance away. The prisoners were in open view and they knew that those who were watching them were using field glasses. But they feared their own troops could not determine with any accuracy that they were actually prisoners.

Zlatomir served in a work group of four men. *Each day we would go out and do almost anything. It was a full day of work for just a little bowl of extra food. We were not allowed to walk around the camp without a pass. When guards or the police came near, we had to pay attention. If they were in a good mood they would greet us and offer a cigarette. If not, you could end up with a blow to the head from a club or a kick between your legs from a boot.*

From one day to the next, life in detention became more routine or "normal," if you could call it that. We had to understand our situation and accept the circumstances. We had to adjust to a new survival mode.

One week the guards assigned to the camp would be from small nearby towns like Grude and Čitluk. The next week they came from Konjic. The rotation of guards was meant to ensure guards and prisoners would not develop a relationship.

The police from Čapljina were stationed at Dretelj but they never came to see those of us who were prisoners from Čapljina. But they did help in one way. Guards were prohibited from mistreating us town folks. They believed that one day after we were released we would all be living together again.

CHAPTER TEN

*A*nd then, the infamous day of July 12, 1993, is a day that every detainee in Dretelj will never forget. It will be remembered forever. On that July day, subversive groups within the Bosnian army based on the Dubrave plateau attacked Croat Army regulars, killing some twenty of them by sneaking up from behind. The attack was likely in response to the arrests of Bosnian civilians in the towns of Buna, Stolac, Čapljina and Ljubuški. They probably believed that action, which came as a surprise to Croats, was very successful. Whoever organized it didn't think about us, five thousand of detainees in Gabela, Dretelj, Ljubuški, Otoci near Vitina, Kočerin, Grude and Posušje. They didn't think about what would happen to us and that we would be the ones to pay for the Croats' revenge, mistreatments, torture, even murders.

The Croatian revenge was savage, quick and brutal. It all started around 9 o'clock in the evening. The first soldiers returned from the front lines and started to terrorize us. We were first told that we wouldn't be given any food or water and that if we went out of the hangar, that we "balije" (a derogatory slur to refer to Muslims) would all be exterminated. They said we would be taken from the hangers and exterminated. They started calling *out civilians from Dubrave, Stolac and Počitelj and beating them until they passed out and more. Until yesterday we were all in the same army, HVO, fighting together with those same soldiers. We were not guilty for what was happening outside. We were guilty of being Muslims – balije.*

This reign of terror continued throughout the entire night. Drunken soldiers, policemen, and men in paramilitary units continued coming in, all with the same goal and desire. They were blood thirsty, as if terrorizing us would make their dead ones return to life. The cries of the injured prisoners echoed throughout the night. Nobody slept that night. People's cries echoed through the night.

The next morning found all of us were extremely anxious.

We didn't know what would happen next.

Ironically, in the case of Zlatomir and probably many others, the mistake was even more profound. Zlatomir was not Muslim. Nobody in his family was Muslim. The grievous error was never clarified.

Early the next day, on July 13, the Croat military began a new round of ethnic cleansing in small towns located on the vast Dubrave Plateau. They were looking for Bosnian men who had escaped the first round of arrests by surreptitiously hiding in forests or home cellars, and other obscure places. Once a man was captured, he was accused of being a subversive member of the Bosnian Army. All of them were brought to the prison camp in small groups and viciously beaten for prolonged periods of time. They were then locked up in Dretelj's solitary confinement in the underground tunnels that burrowed beneath the prison camp. The tunnels had been dug by miners a very long time ago.

We learned about the horror that occurred in Buna, Stolac and Dubrave from survivors of those towns who ended up in our prison camp. Croats were not satisfied in just arresting and torturing men. They started in on women, children and the elderly in those regions.

The Croats expelled and deported everyone considered to be Bosnian. The road to Blagaj grew into an exodus of humanity. Within days, every Muslim in the entire area who had not already been deported was walking towards Blagaj. Homes were sacked and burned, hundreds of people were killed and many young women were viciously raped, dying later of internal injuries. All signs of Muslim heritage were destroyed, including eleven mosques that were levelled to the ground. Of the one thousands mosques in country at the start of the war, fewer than one hundred survived the carnage.

The days between July 13 and 16, later dubbed "the days of punishment," were the worst. Survivors will never forget them.

We were so crammed together into such small spaces that some men were forced to lie on top of one another because there was no other room. We were hungry, thirsty, exhausted and without hope. We were dying. They were killing us slowly. Somehow we endured day after day but young boys, some as young as 13 years, and old men over 60 years struggled the worst. There was not enough water and what little we had was always given to them first. The rest of us would sip a bottle cap of water, just enough to wet our lips.

Adding to the torment, irate and quite possibly deranged guards began shooting once again into the barracks with machine guns. Bullets ricochet everywhere. Five hundred men were crammed into the space. One bullet hit the leg of a man in the middle of the hanger. His lower leg was broken in half. Others were wounded. Guards eventually opened the hanger doors and allowed the prisoners to carry the injured to an infirmary in the camp. The infirmary was terrible. Medical personnel worked non-stop in horrible, filthy and crowded conditions. There were two or three patients in each bed and others were lying on the floor.

The men in our hangar were lucky compared to those in other hangars. The hangar next to us was shot at with automatic weapons. Bullets flew through the thin walls. Thirty-five men were wounded. Those who were seriously injured were transferred out of the camp. We never learned where they went and we never knew what became of them.

A number of men locked into the underground tunnels died from severe beatings. They were transported out of the camp and buried in remote regions near the small towns of Počitelj and Bivolje Brdo. Nobody, according to Zlatomir, will ever know the exact number of those whose lives ended in death, just because they were Muslim or thought to be Muslim.

Our greatest fear was from the guards who threatened to throw hand grenades into our hanger. If they did, we knew it would be devastating because the area was so small and filled with so many men. But they were just threats, part of the psychological war on us. The guards were terrorizing people who were already half dead.

Adding to the terror were threats by local policemen who came into the camp without advanced warning. They came for a single reason, to mistreat and torture the prisoners. Ančić, commander of the military police in Dretelj, did not restrict nor even restrain policemen or HVO soldiers under his command who made a practice of such macabre activity.

On July 17, prisoners were allowed one meal and one sip of water in the afternoon.

We were relieved, thinking the situation was maybe quieting down a bit. The next day they gave us more water and thirty-three regular meals for three thousand people. When it was our turn to eat, we were each given ten seconds to swallow the food, if that is what you would call it. It was more like mush. A small loaf of bread was divided into 16 slices.

We had to crouch low and run to grab the food, swallowing the mush quickly and then rise and run back to the hangars. The food was scalding hot. On more than one occasion, I only had time to eat a spoonful or two before running for cold water and leaving most of the ration behind. Scalding food and cold water a terrible combination. We were content with whatever was given to us.

Every prisoner was worried about contracting a contagious disease. Many among us were sick, suffering from tuberculosis and many other serious diseases. We all ate from a single spoon and leftover food was always added to and mixed into pots of new food. Diarrhoea was frequent and in the beginning we had no medicine to treat anything. Many men suffered from lice, scabies and other skin diseases. My brother and I were lucky because we did not catch any of these things.

Those in solitary confinement were especially brutalized by treatment the guards referred to as "special." Prisoners thought to be members of the Bosnian Army or suspected of supporting the Bosnian Army were held in solitary confinement, in the caves below the camps. They were tortured daily. During meal times, they were fed last. To even get food they had to run a gauntlet between two rows of policemen armed with clubs that they viciously swung. When prisoners finally reached the food and were allowed to eat, guards hit them alongside the head with ladles used to serve the food.

Another favourite form of brutality was forcing the prisoners to undress and lie naked on hot asphalt. They sustained painful burns on the parts of their body that touched the asphalt. Guards wearing military boots would run back and forth over the naked bodies of the men who were lying on the asphalt.

Zlatomir's brother, Miro, was once inadvertently caught up in "special" treatment. *On a typical hot day in summer, Miro was sitting on the ground with a group of men. A guard motioned in his direction. Miro asked if the guard meant him. "You'll do," he was told. The guard was a young, inexperienced, man intent on a bit of "fun." Miro was ordered to remove his shirt and then forced to lay face up on the hot asphalt. Anyone who has tried to walk barefoot on hot asphalt knows that under the heat of the day's sun, asphalt can reach excessively high temperatures. Prolonged contact causes severe burns. By the time Miro was finally returned to the barracks, his back and chest were painfully burned.* "Quite red," Zlatomir observed, as he tried to nurse Miro with the poor medical supplies available to him.

Another form of prisoner harassment was forcing them to stand in long lines facing barrack walls for extended periods of time. They were ordered to raise their hands above their head. Then they had had to repeatedly sing two Ustashe songs that were especially derogatory to Muslims, "Jure and Boban Are Coming" and "I Don't Love You Alia Because You're Balia (Muslim)." Standing with their arms stretched high overhead and singing loudly, the guards walked along the line of prisoners hitting them with bats, large sticks and even shovels. Facing the wall, the prisoners could neither anticipate the blows nor ward them off.

On one particular day we prisoners were forced to face a wall that formed one side of the barracks. The men inside could hear every sound of the repetitious singing, mixed with the loud smacks of blows on bare skin and finally, desperate cries of agony. Those inside were threatened with a bullet to the head if they dared look out the small barrack window to see what was happening to their comrade prisoners.

Torture, singing and loud smacks were constant daily events. The pitiful camp infirmary was constantly full of victims who were injured in the attacks. Once an injured man regained the slightest semblance of health, he was immediately returned to the barracks where the mistreatment started all over again.

Not only were Croat police and guards terrorizing us, but local Muslims who had somehow escaped arrest joined in and became a part of the mistreatment, Zlatomir said.

They were seeking favour, doing terrible things to us by kissing Croat ass. These Muslims were very exacting in their disagreeable and ugly duties. They would relentlessly beat us. Those I remember most were Trebinjac, Senad Bešić and Mara, whose last name was Marić. I don't know his full name but he was Joca Jovanović's brother-in-law.

Days passed in numbed silence. Nights were the worst because prisoners anticipated and imagined both mistreatment and beatings the following day by police, guards and local men who were allowed to take prisoners at will from their cells for "a bit of fun."

On August 13, there were many battles around Mostar that likely resulted in numerous Croat casualties.

When something like that happened, we normally paid for it. This time it was no different. Over four long days we received only one meal a day and we were continuously tortured, both physically and psychologically. At that time we were under the control of the Konjic Police twenty-four hours a day. Their treatment of us was based on what was happening in Mostar,

Konjic, Jablanica, Prozor or any other town in Central Bosnia that had became a battlefield. It all depended on Bosnian successes or Croat failures.

Croat forces simultaneously completed ethnic cleansing in many of the smaller communities adjacent to Čapljina. They included Stolac, Dubrave, Višići, Čeljevo and Počitelj. The residents of those towns were either deported to Blagaj or to other places on the left bank of the Neretva River that was still under control of the Bosnian Army. But the town of Čapljina was never invaded.

A rumor made the rounds. A new warden had been assigned to Dretelj, a man by the name of Tomo Šakota. He was from the nearby town of Čitluk and he was a well-known football star who had once been a prisoner in Foča. Prisoners hoped that a man who had been subjected to harsh brutality as a prisoner would treat them more decently.

Šakota arrived in Dretelj ten days later and at first we felt a difference. We started receiving a second meal each day and one loaf of bread was divided into only nine slices. The guards were ordered to lock the hangers at night and for safekeeping, the keys were locked up in the warden's office. Guards would no longer have access to us during the night and they could no longer take us outside for "fun" or torture. We liked the new warden because he helped many of us. He allowed us to phone our families and tell them where we were and how we were. It was the first time many families had heard from their sons, husbands and brothers since the start of the mass arrests. Detainees began to receive letters from family members and others. Some were even released from camp.

Not everything, however, improved. The more humane treatment and other better conditions soon lapsed. The guards again continued their "fun" without constraint and without any oversight.

One night a group of old men over 60 years of age, and youths 18 years and younger, were rounded up in camp, loaded onto the back of the trucks and driven to the Croat-Bosnian line of demarcation in the town of Buna. What at first might have been a prisoner transfer or exchange proved to be something quite different and much more onerous. When the trucks pulled to a stop at a predetermined destination, prisoners were forced from the trucks and made to strip naked. Then, they were made to run over a field of buried land mines. Soldiers began shooting, aiming at the men and forcing both the old and the young to run as fast as possible over the dangerous ground.

Patients from the local asylum for the mentally ill were also forced into the macabre race. The mentally ill and prisoners in poor physical condition were forced to run as fast as they could over unknown territory that was deadly. Run for your life!

We later learned that many of those forced into the running were wounded and others were killed. Guards did whatever they wanted to us without interference. Then, they made certain there was no remaining evidence that could possibly hold them accountable and later result in criminal charges.

Hope increased when prisoners learned representatives of the International Red Cross would soon visit the camp. Each detainee was to be registered as a prisoner of war during the visit.

Before the Red Cross came into the prison camp, the guards asked us who speaks a second language, so everyone who claimed to speak a second language was taken away and we never saw them again. The guards were afraid that prisoners could talk in another language would tell the truth of what was really going on in the prison camp to the Red Cross and journalists.

Our names would be entered into an official record. After what we had experienced until then, the upcoming visit and registration by the Red Cross was seen as some sort of a guarantee on life. We were relieved when the Red Cross arrived. Everyone was registered.

Other visitors followed on the heels of the Red Cross. Journalists and television crews arrived, both from local stations and abroad, including crews from throughout Europe and the United States.

Finally, photos of us would be broadcast. The world would learn about Dretelj, this hell on earth. Prisoners in Dretelj believed their camp was among the most brutal, far more terrible than camps in other towns such as Manjač and Bileća. They were nothing compared to Dretelj.

One particular photo that appeared in print around the world most vividly carried the message about the brutality in Bosnian prison camps. A man who is rail thin, thinner than can even be imagined holds his emaciated outstretched arm towards a chain link fence. He is steadying himself so as to not fall. His rib cage clearly protrudes from beneath a layer of filthy skin. He is obviously in the advanced stages of starvation. The photo created an international uproar over the condition of the camps that, until then, were not widely known beyond Bosnia. The international outcry forced an immediate response from the country's leaders. Something had to be done, and quickly!

Among those who visited Dretelj then was Armin Pohara, president of a Muslim party. He was accompanied by Rusmir Mahmutčehajić on the visit.

Pohara promised us he would intervene and urged the Croats to improve our conditions by supplying us with blankets. We would be freed, he said, as soon as the war ended. That should be very soon. We booed him because we knew why he had come. He was not representing Muslims at all. He was representing himself. We suggested he visit the left bank of Mostar which had been bombed into oblivion. He rejected our suggestion because he knew what he would find.

Red Cross representatives visited a second time, providing each prisoner a sweat suit and coat, a bar of soap and shampoo, washing detergent and a pack of cigarettes. Journalists interviewed detainees and snapped photographs. "We were breathing again," Zlatomir recalls. "The journalists asked many questions but there really was no need. Our situation spoke for itself. We were talking skeletons. Some guys lost more than fifty kilos (110 pounds). My brother and I each lost twenty-six kilos (57 pounds), as did many others."

Again, Red Cross workers promised the prisoners freedom, as soon as politicians struck a deal. Our unit was getting smaller. Prisoners married to Bosnian women of Croat or Serb background were among the first to be released.

Every time someone left, they promised to send us food and other things that would ease our situation. But these were empty words. Prisoners might be freed from prison but they could not obtain passes for travel around the country. They were free but it was as good as being under house arrest.

In addition, there was another caveat for release. Before release from camp, each man had to pledge conversion to the Catholic religion. Although the majority of prisoners professed no religious ties, becoming Catholic was a requirement in order to be released from prison camp.

New collisions between the HVO and the Bosnian Army in Mostar, Dubrave and central Bosnia erupted on September 13. As expected, the prisoners had problems with the police who employed the same tactics as before. They usually attacked us in the dark of night. These new waves of repression usually lasted for three days each. Over the next three months, the same mistreatment occurred on the same date.

Was that just coincidence? Coincidence or not, we remembered the beatings and even more, we felt them.

After the original visit, the Red Cross returned to the camp one week later. They weighed each of the prisoners, adding new numbers to their meticulous lists of growing records. Finally, on Sept 29 a group of five hundred and forty detainees were released. They were sent to recover on the island of Badija, near by the island of Korčula.

We were very happy for them and we read meaning into what it might mean for the rest of us. Because so many were released, it might mean something was really happening outside.

At the very least, someone was thinking about us, the remaining prisoners.

The following day a delegation led by Granić, the Deputy Prime Minister, came to visit those still in the camps. He said a deal for our release was in the works between him and Silajdžić, the Minister of Foreign Affairs. It meant the rest of us would soon be free and the camp would be permanently closed. He was only half right.

Later in the day guards arrived to free us but we were tricked. Instead of being set free, we were transferred to a second war camp in (the town of) Gabela. The entire thing with Granić had been a ruse, noting more than a bad word game. Croatian newspapers wrote about us being transferred to the refugee camps in Obanjanje and Gašinci in Croatia; some wrote we were on the island of Pag; others wrote we were taken to Varaždinske Toplice. All lies. Telling lies to the entire world.

We were transported to Gabela and everyone from Dretelj was locked up in one hanger, nearly five hundred of us. We had heard all kinds of stories about this camp in Gabela and now we had a chance to verify them. The warden was called Boko. He was an extreme nationalist and known to be crazy. The moment we arrived in Gabela he started lecturing us about the rules of the camp, the "do's" and the "don'ts." We could not leave the hanger. Food would be brought to us and we had to eat where we slept. We could not smoke or have canned food in our possession.

To maintain the rules, Previšić ordered many surprise raids on the barracks. Guards would confiscate our cans of food and cigarettes. The next day they would sell them back to anyone lucky enough to still have money hidden away. Then, the next day they would confiscate everything again, just to sell the same things back to us the day after. This went on day after day. Those who volunteered for work duty were sent to the military base in Čapljina, where they laboured the entire day for a single pack of cigarettes or an extra piece of bread.

One day in early October, a young man by the name of Obradović tried to sneak a piece of bread back into camp.

He was nineteen years old. He hid the bread under a shabby belt he used to hold up his pants. Boko and his men raided the hanger after we had settled in. Boko took the bread from Obradović and then from a distance of two meters shot him. Astonishingly, Boko missed. Then he grabbed an automatic weapon from a soldier standing nearby and shot Obradović again. This was in front of everyone, both detainees and soldiers. Obradović's body lay where it fell for two days. Someone covered it with a blanket. Then finally, the body was taken away and, I guess, buried.

Boko, who was known to be both incompetent and crazy, was not held responsible then for any of his actions. He was not accountable to anyone. He was just what the detainees needed, men who were already fighting for survival.

Six days later a man from the town of Stolac named Bešo was also murdered. He was forty years old and on a work detail outside of camp at the military base in Čapljina. Without provocation, a drunken soldier wielding a pistol shot him to death. There was no reason for the shooting, no provocation. Again, nothing was done to discipline the soldier who murdered Bešo.

"It was clear that the life of a detainee was not worth a dime."

CHAPTER ELEVEN

The most profound moment in the life of Zlatomir Šarić happened on a dry, brisk day in late November 1993. Without warning or explanation, he was suddenly released from a dreadful makeshift prison camp near the small Bosnian town of Gabela in central Europe. He had been held there under terrible conditions for six months and had long despaired this day would ever arrive.

Gabela, at this time of year, was bathed golden-red by scores of autumn leaves silently dropping from old forests of oak and spruce. But, the bucolic scene belied the intensity of the moment. Four years earlier a vicious civil war had erupted when Croatian and Serbian troops invaded the smaller nation of Bosnia. Many, like Zlatomir, were captured during the bloody conflict and held by the enemy as prisoners of war.

Zlatomir quickly walked through the sturdy gates at the entry of the camp. His heart quickened. Standing before him were a sister and her husband, relatives he thought he might never see again. During the mean months of incarceration, he had heard nothing from his family. Like all the prisoners, he had relied on rumors as the only source of information about the current state of Bosnia and the world at large. Zlatomir had never even been certain that his family knew he was a prisoner and if they did know, they wouldn't know where he was detained.

On October 17, 1993, to our shock and disbelief, my sister Zijada and her husband Zvonko, my brother in law, entered the camp and that is where we met. Nobody until then even imagined in their dreams that civilians would be allowed to come close to the camp, let alone to get in. And there they were. Zvonko later told us he had pulled all of the political strings he had to get us out of there and he hoped that it would happen soon.

The following day there was a huge exchange of some six hundred prisoners who volunteered to go to Jablanica. Within several more days, there was to be another exchange and these detainees would be sent to Mostar. But this exchange was delayed many times.

On the twenty-first Zvonko again entered Gabela, he had returned a second time to get us. He had managed to secure all the necessary papers.

We are out! We are free! We can hardly believe this is for real. We ran breathless through the gates. We don't think. Our legs are moving. We didn't even feel them. We got in the car with Zvonko and he took both my brother and me to our apartments in Čapljina. When I first entered my apartment, it was empty and dead. I am sure it belonged to someone else.

We had been given two hours to get out of town so we hurried. We took a quick shower and left for Dalmacija stopping by our old aunt's house for a quick good-bye. This is the same aunt who later shared an apartment with Zlatomir's mother in the State of Washington.

Prior to Zlatomir's release there had been an earlier prisoner exchange that Zlatomir could have been part of. But his relatives discouraged him from taking part. He would have been relocated to southern Bosnia Hercegovina. It was too close to home and his relatives feared for his safety there.

"My sister was afraid for me to stay in Bosnia. I was very angry and my family feared that if I stayed in the country, there would be an incident. I might seek revenge." Zlatomir agreed. "It is better if I stay (in prison) longer and then choose where I go. It is better for me to suffer a little longer but go where I want. If I stay in Bosnia, they will kill me for sure." So Zlatomir patiently bided his time and waited for a prisoner release to Croatia and later, to the United States.

Zlatomir's unexpected release brought to a stunning end, a dark chapter that began for him during the treacherous civil war raging throughout Bosnia between 1992 and 1995. Zlatomir, a Bosnian by both birth and residency, had enlisted in the Croat army. Bosnia and Croatia were then political allies, fighting together in the war against an aggressive Serbia. The Croat Army was the most powerful military force in the region and everyone expected it to be victorious. But Bosnia suddenly found itself abandoned by Croatia and other Balkan neighbors that for political reasons sided with Serbia, the country that was attacking Bosnia. Bosnia became a Balkan orphan.

The nation was one of six new republics that emerged during the great internal strife that engulfed the region for nearly four years. Bosnia is a small nation sandwiched between Croatia and Serbia in Central Europe. In 1991 Bosnia was recognized as an independent republic and seated at the United Nations.

Once war erupted, Zlatomir faced few options other than enlisting in the military. All men between sixteen and sixty years of age were expected to serve and eventually every man did. By volunteering for service, Zlatomir was able to select where he wanted to serve in Bosnia. He opted for the Čapljina area. Otherwise, he was certain to be drafted, which meant he could face assignment anywhere in the country where he was most needed.

Millions of words have been written about the Bosnian conflict, the reasons that caused it, the impact in that part of the world, and the outcome of the war. But little of the literature concerns the ordinary fighter; the average men from modest homes who helped defend their country from enemies who were former friends, class-mates and comrades.

Zlatomir was arrested on the first day of July in 1993, after having served only six months in the military. It was an especially frenzied time, when scores of men were apprehended simply be-cause of their Bosnian heritage. They were identified by family name and arrested by comrades who only days before had been in the same military units. Men were snatched off the streets of town or from nearby battlefields. Although people of both Croatian and Bosnian heritage had lived peacefully as neighbors for as long as anyone in this generation could remember, they had now become bitter enemies divided by religion, politics and above all, revenge.

"The army arrested everyone they believed didn't think like them. But we were all Bosnian," Zlatomir said, in an effort to ex-plain the confusing situation. It is complex because of the many mixed nationalities that live in Bosnia and who fought in the war. Intermarriage between people of Bosnian, Serbian and Croatian heritage was common. Nobody in Zlatomir's generation had ever paid it more than a passing thought.

The arrests were a treachery of epic proportion, a stark in-stance of blatant political betrayal. Men serving in the same mili-tary do not expect to be arrested by their own comrades, especially during the heat of battle and for reasons as flimsy as heritage. It is simply unfathomable to most. The arrested men were held under appalling conditions in brutal camps run by Bosnians of Croat heritage that were former acquaintances, and by Croat forces that had invaded Bosnia earlier in the year. Prison camps now dotted the lush Bosnia countryside, comparing in brutality to the notori-ous Nazi-era concentration camps of World War II.

When Zlatomir was arrested, he was a tall strong and fit man nearly forty years old. But by the time of his release six months lat-er, he had dramatically changed. Now he was rail thin and gaunt.

He had lost considerable weight. He never knew exactly how much he weighed either before or after, but now he needed a belt to hold up pants he had comfortably worn just a short time before. His hair had been shorn and his shock of thick dark hair was now little more than patches of white stubble. His gums were sore, his teeth loose. A large mass protruded from his abdomen, the likely result of an injury from the hard labor forced upon prisoners who were surviving on near-starvation diets. He eventually required surgery to repair a massive intestinal tear.

But Zlatomir described the source of most discomfort as "rough meat," the thick, raw calluses that marked parts of his body that had pressed too long against unforgiving concrete floors. Prisoners were crammed together into spaces much too small for so many and forced to sit without moving for long hours at a time, simply slumping over onto hard cement to sleep. Their slightest move-ment provoked harsh punishment from the guards. Unprotected areas of Zlatomir's body, his hips and shoulders, ankles and wrists, became masses of seeping sores.

Recalling that terrible time nearly twenty years later, Zlatomir insists he was not in pain. "Actually, I didn't feel much of any-thing,' he said in thick European-accented English. "It's like my body was no longer my own." He often pauses in describing the experience and must be urged to continue. Bosnian men are generally reluctant to discuss personal issues, especially some-thing as sensitive as this. Zlatomir only speaks now in response to pertinent questions.

A wad of cash secured the release of both Zlatomir and his brother Miro, called Pop, three years older than him. Both of them had been arrested on the streets of their hometown within a day of the other, and both were held in the same prison sys-tem. An older sister and her husband drove three hours from their home in Croatia to secure their release, paying camp command-ers the princely sum of one thousand dollars for each brother, a total of two thousand dollars. The couple seemingly had the right credentials for the task. Although both had been born and raised in Bosnia, their last name was of Croatian derivation and they had lived for years in a modest Croatian town where they were raising a family.

Money was deftly slipped into the outstretched hands of greedy camp officials who were accustomed to bribes. Then, Red Cross prisoners 352514 and 352515, the Šarić brothers, were set free. The long days of deprivation and abuse were over. All that lingered was the fear.

"My only thought was I wanted to get as far away from that terrible place as fast as I could. I didn't ever want to see it again. I told myself 'Go. Don't look back. Don't stop. Just run. Run away.' And Zlatomir did, running as fast as his weakened condition allowed, down the sloping gravel path. He feared tripping over his own feet, slipping and falling before he could reach the safety of the car parked below.

"I'll never forget that moment!" Zlatomir recalls it as the most intense emotion he has ever felt, either before or since.

Stern guards threatened: "You have two hours to disappear for good. Or else!" The brothers scrambled into the car and sped away, stopping only briefly in Čapljina where Zlatomir experienced his first stroke of good luck in some time. During his absence, Zlatomir's apartment home had not been ransacked and enemy soldiers were not living in it. Most of Zlatomir's possessions were exactly as he had left them. The only thing missing was his dog Aphrodite, a female Lassie he had named after the Greek goddess of love. The animal was outside when Zlatomir was arrested. There had been no opportunity to arrange care for her. He never saw the dog again. Nor did he ever learn her fate.

Zlatomir quickly showered away months of stink and grime and then dressed in the same filthy, olive-green prison uniform provided him months before by the International Red Cross. He never thought to open the door to his closet for a set of clean clothes.

"I don't know why," he explained. "But when I walked into my place I felt like a stranger. It just didn't feel like it was my home. Nothing was mine anymore." At that moment, Zlatomir was disconnected from a past that seemed hazy and remote. The months in prison had effectively severed any sense of his past. There was no life before war, no home. Even his clothes had become strange to him.

The car holding the small group headed southwest past sparkling lakes and spruce woods, quickly descending switchbacks on the twisting mountain road. They finally reached the relative safety of the sister's home on the Adriatic coast in Croatia. Except for brief shelling a year before, there were few signs of war in the area and the coast remained relatively safe. A fragile truce held the peace.

Zlatomir spent the next three months with his sister, gaining lost weight on his sister's home cooking and anxiously waiting for a safe exit visa out of Croatia.

When I finally got out of prison camp I was hiding in plain sight because they can shoot you or send you to a different prison camp. Nobody knew who I was when I would walk along the beach during the day. The night swallows you. Many people would disappear at night and would be found dead floating in the water. The paramilitary groups would search at night for released Bosnian prisoners, even if they had protection papers from the Red Cross. I was just bull shit these papers of protection. Nothing but your own intelligence could save you. We were still fair game. It was war and it was hell.

During the day he paced the meandering shoreline of the Adriatic Sea, walking thousands of steps in the sand, up and down and back and forth. The walking calmed him, serving as a tonic for his ailing spirit. Once in the safety of his sister's home, the haunting memories of war and prison slowly began to recede, replaced with the first stirrings of hope and emotional health. In the evenings he spent hours jotting down the horrendous memories in what became his journal. It was therapeutic and he hoped that the names and faces of those that had brutalized and imprisoned him would one day be revealed to the world.

CHAPTER TWELVE

Millions of words have been written about the Bosnian conflict, the reasons that caused it, the impact in that part of the world, and the outcome of the war. But little of the literature concerns the ordinary fighter; the average men from modest homes who helped defend their country from enemies who were former friends, classmates and comrades.

War disrupted this picturesque pastoral region in the final months of the 1990's when terrible strife, tension and threats exploded into a bloody confrontation variously called the Bosnian War or the War of Bosnia-Hercegovina. Bosnia-Hercegovina is one of six regions in the country and it is surrounded by Croatia on one side and Serbia on the other.

Before the war ended nearly four years later, millions in this Balkan nation lost everything. An estimated 100,000 people were killed, including many women, children and old men. Another 175,000 were wounded. Some 50,000 young girls, old grandmothers and countless teen boys were raped. "Ethnic cleansing," a phrase hardly known at the start of the war, grew into common usage to describe an especially harsh tactic of war in which cities and towns were entirely razed. Rare archeological and historical sites were destroyed and ancient mosques were burned to the ground. Ten thousand men died in concentration camps, evoking memories of World War II. Another 10,000 people remain missing to this day, including over 1,000 children. There is little hope of discovering their remains or ever learning their fate.

Some twenty years later the journal assumed renewed importance when Zlatomir began to expand the original account into a fuller story. The project posed enormous challenges for him, including a precarious emotional journey into a dreadful past. Zlatomir had to dredge up from the past an experience he had carefully blocked from memory because "it was so bad." In the beginning, he experienced a foreboding that eventually became mild depression for a brief period.

"It was like revisiting hell," Zlatomir said, "a ruthless place filled with vile threats, harsh treatment and the screams of prisoners who were already half dead. The worst part was feeling helpless as relatives, friends and colleagues slowly deteriorated.

Once strong men, they were slowly reduced to pitiful skeletons. Life slipped away by inches each day. Then the dying began. Indifferent prison guards, who had known the prisoners from before, looked on with disinterest. They were now considered enemies."

Zlatomir was luckier than many veterans of the war who decades later continue to suffer nightmares and flashbacks. Therapists still treat former prisoners of the Serbian and Croatian camps, helping them cope with trauma. For many, it seems to be an almost elusive, futile battle.

In prison, Zlatomir memorized every detail he considered significant. He filed away memories by silently repeating the same facts to himself over and over again. He volunteered to work outside the barracks at every opportunity, performing such menial tasks as pulling weeds or collecting trash. The moments provided him quiet time when he memorized anything he considered important about the camp. He relied on word triggers to call up the names of individual guards and dates of significance. Whether he was raking the grounds or hauling garbage, he continuously muttered, committing to memory details of the dreadful ordeal.

"I wanted to remember what happened. I didn't want to forget anything. I wanted to remember every detail."

Zlatomir began writing about the experience while waiting for an exit visa out of his former country. He jotted down his thoughts into a thick tablet. The pages quickly multiplied, growing into a makeshift manuscript. It was Zlatomir's intimate journal, a detailed and precise version of a treacherous time.

During his first return visit to the country, he experienced a rush of strong emotion. *We see people in the streets but we don't recognize anybody. Čapljina is no longer the town it used to be. My town is no longer my town, and it will never be mine again. Now there are only strangers. Those who were the very heart of the town are now in exile. A small number of Croats remain. Those who have stayed are decent people. They hide in their apartments because there is nobody left to hang out with or to visit. Their friends have fled and now there is no one left to share their lives with. I hope the time will eventually come when they can speak to the authorities and say, "Give us back our Muslims!"*

Zlatomir has returned home for visits to Čapljina a half-dozen times. What he has seen leaves him pessimistic about Bosnia's future. He is not hopeful. "There is still too much hate." More importantly, he believes no leader has emerged who is strong enough or capable of "pulling everyone together" into a single cohesive unit that can function in a healthy way.

Of Zlatomir's four close friends from Čapljina who originally formed a mini-militia unit, all were eventually arrested and imprisoned in concentration camps. Only Troko and Zlatomir ended up in the same camp. Žane remained free the longest, by hiding in the forest on the river island of Ada. He surrendered after authorities arrested his teen son. He traded his own freedom for that of his son.

On a return visit to his hometown of Čapljina in the summer of 2009, Zlatomir realized that this was no longer "my place." He had spent forty years in the town but now, nearly twenty years later, he felt like a stranger. He said that when walking the streets he recognized many people. He spoke to few of them, believing they had abandoned him and the others during hard times. He said he feels eyes of the guilty on him. He believes they feel shame, peering at him from behind drawn window curtains.

Zlatomir believes they are people who more than likely did not support the arrest of him and the others. Still, they never offered a helping hand. If they had, of course, they would have jeopardized their own freedom and that of their families. At that time, nearly everyone knew the arrests were little more than political moves. No one was willing to speak up. They knew it would have been useless to do so. The arrests were simply politics in that place, at that time. Zlatomir speculates: "I bet they hate themselves now. I bet they are in hell."

The Šarić family suffered their fair share. In a scramble for safety, the family scattered to different parts of the world, relocating far from one another, even to separate continents. The family has never had opportunity to gather as one since and long periods of time between visits have frayed family ties. But they now forge contact by phone or, more recently, the Internet. Still, long periods of silence have weakened family ties.

Zlatomir's mother, already an elderly woman in her 80s when war began, was spirited abroad to safety in the United States where she eventually died without seeing many of her children and grandchildren a final time. An older brother, a retired university professor who continues to live in Sarajevo with his wife, perhaps suffered most. His only child, an adult daughter working in Western Europe, was home in Bosnia on annual leave when war began. She was unable to find a way out of the country. While standing in line for water with her mother, she was killed by a bomb explosion. Years later, a new species of flower discovered just outside Sarajevo was named in her honor, the 'Jasna.' It is a fragile lavender blossom that once earned Best of Show in a floral competition hosted by China.

The eldest brother whom Zlatomir last saw years ago, fled with his family to Denmark where he raised a family and continues to live. If the two passed on the street, it is unlikely they would recognize each another because it has been so many years since the two last saw one other. Another brother took his chances and with his family stayed in Sarajevo where a son-in-law was killed by a grenade. A brother, who now lives in the United States, escaped like thousands before him by crawling with his young family through underground tunnels dug by hand under the airport runway in Sarajevo.

The two youngest brothers, Zlatomir and Miro, lost years of their lives, first fighting in a terrible war and then fighting to survive in dreadful prison camps where they were subjected to emotional and physical torment. Both later resettled in Seattle where Miro unexpectedly died in 2013. Zlatomir was devastated by his brother's death. Miro was scheduled to visit Zlatomir in Phoenix the following week after his death. Both were greatly anticipating the visit.

Zlatomir's oldest sister had already died in childbirth before the war. Two remaining sisters escaped the brunt of violence by living in small towns that were almost entirely free of fighting. The youngest lived in Croatia and later figured large in the lives of the two youngest brothers when they were incarcerated in prison camps near her home. The older sister lives in Serbia. A protective husband told her little of the war, shielding her from the news. But once he died, she seized the opportunity to learn more. When her youngest brother visited many years later, she pressed him for details. Listening to Zlatomir's story, she held her head in her hands and rocked back and forth.

Once Zlatomir left Bosnia for good in November 1993, he did not return to the country for 7 years. In 2002 on his first visit to his old home, he and a sister placed flowers on the graves of their parents in the Čapljina cemetery. On the walk home to the family apartment where an elderly aunt now lived, Zlatomir met his former neighbor on the street. It was the same man who had ignored Zlatomir's plight and offered no assistance during his time of most need. The man was now much older and stooped. He smiled a greeting but Zlatomir walked past without acknowledgment. The neighbor's betrayal still stung.

As soon as possible after receiving formal emigration papers, Zlatomir, Tuca and Dragan left for the United States where Dragan died of lung cancer in 1997, shortly after arriving. Tuca continues to live in Idaho. Žane immigrated to Germany where he died of a heart attack in 2005. Troko remains in Bosnia and lives in Mostar with his family. Following the end of the war, the original group of friends never reunited. Some, like Dragan and Žane, never even saw one another again before dying early at young ages.

Skype has dramatically altered the situation for the remaining survivors. They now maintain regular Internet contact, and have even widened their circle to include additional friends who are veterans and who are joining the site from various locations throughout the world.

On a return visit to his hometown of Čapljina in the summer of 2009, Zlatomir realized that this was no longer "my place." He had spent forty years in the town but now, nearly twenty years later, he felt like a stranger. He said that when walking the streets he recognized many people. He spoke to few of them, believing they had abandoned him and the others during hard times. He said he feels eyes of the guilty on him. He believes they feel shame, peering at him from behind drawn window curtains.

We see people in the streets but we don't recognize anybody. Čapljina is no longer the town it used to be. My town is no longer my home.

In May 2012, a mass funeral was conducted in Višegrad for sixty-six Muslim Bosnians killed by Bosnian Serb forces during the war. The victims' remains were discovered only two years earlier, when a man-made lake dividing Bosnia from Serbia was partially drained for the maintenance of a dam on the lake. The remains were identified through DNA analysis.

Several weeks later the Dutch Supreme Court rejected an attempt by relatives of Bosnian Muslim men murdered by Serb forces to sue the United Nations for failure to protect them during a massacre in Srebrenica in July 1995. Most were slain in summary executions. U.N. peacekeepers were undermanned and outgunned, and failed to intervene The Netherlands' highest court ruled the United Nations enjoyed immunity from prosecution.

Mothers of Srebrenica organized in 1996 and since then the women have labored to identify the remains of loved ones who were victimized. Their goal is to bring perpetrators of the crimes to justice. Every woman in the group lost at least one member of her family to massacres, including 10,700 men, 5,070 women and 1,042 children.

In May 2012, Bosnia's war-crimes court convicted four Bosnian soldiers of Serbian heritage and sentenced them to a total of 142 years in prison for the execution of hundreds of Srebrenica Muslims. Some eight hundred captured Muslim Bosnians were shot and killed at Branjevo military farm near Srebrenica. Nearly eight thousand men and boys were held there. All of them were either murdered or died of starvation.

In early 2012, it seemed little had been learned from the war. Ultranationalist Tomislav Nikolić, once a close ally of Milošević, the man who had rained horror in Bosnia, was elected president of Serbia. To chants of "Tomo the Serb," Nikolić ran on a populist platform, criticizing widespread social injustice and corruption in Serbia. He promised both new jobs and financial security. He said his staunchly anti-Western stance had shifted and he is now pro-European Union. Political pundits caution that Nikolic's win could increase political turmoil and slow Serbia's attempts to join the European Union.

Author Misha Glenny wrote of Zlatomir's hometown in 1992 that "towns like Čapljina which straddle the Neretva River have sustained some of the worst destruction (in the war) and it is hard to imagine how life in Čapljina can ever be restored." The destruction came from Serbs attacking east of town, while Croats attacked from the west.

Zlatomir disagrees with Glenny's description. The town certainly suffered damaged and some areas were even heavily bombarded. But it was the smaller, nearby hamlets that were obliterated. Families lost everything. Following the end of hostilities. Čapljina was restored in record time.

Zlatomir jokes with a dark humor that after writing about the war and naming names, he may never again freely walk the streets of Čapljina. He has exposed many names involved in questionable activities during wartime that, until now, have remained well hidden.

Nobody misses prison camp or talks fondly about it. But when the veterans are all together in social setting, it seems as though all they want to talk about is the war and the prison camps.

Since becoming a naturalized citizen in 1999, Zlatomir has never missed voting in a presidential election. The first presidential candidate he ever voted for was Bill Clinton. He considers voting to be a grave privilege. While many if not most people run to the polls during a spare moment in the day, Zlatomir carefully prepares for the event. He is quite possibly the only person waiting in line who has dressed into a suit expressly for the occasion. To him, it is the "respectful" way to cast a vote.

Zlatomir's elderly mother traveled on an airplane for the first time in her 80's, flying to Seattle where three of her sons then living with their families. She and an elderly sister shared an apartment in Washington State until the old woman died at age 94 in 2004. Her sister returned to Bosnia. Neither of the elderly women ever learned to speak English.

Following the Bosnia Herzegovina war, Bosnian emigration to the United States increased dramatically. The numbers have nearly tripled, from nearly 90,000 in the U.S. Census of 1990, to some 350,000 Bosnian Americans today. Many of them, some 70,000, live in Chicago and the South End of Hartland, Connecticut, is commonly referred to as Bosnian Square. New York City hosts an annual Bosnian-Hercegovina film festival. A Bosnian language newspaper, Sabah, is published in St. Louis and BosTel, the first Bosnian American TV channel serving the Bosnian diaspora in North America. Religious associations are active in cities throughout the United States.

Zlatomir worked and lived in Seattle for thirteen years until he decided he had had enough of the constant rain. While he lived in Washington he championed for the children of Yugoslavia who continue to be victims of war and are injured and killed in the minefields left over from the war. "When I visit my country it hurts my heart when I see what happens to the children who play and they find the minefields. And it's still happening. The children find the undetonated grenades and mines."

Zlatomir's passion to provide for these innocent victims of a war not of their making, the disabled and less fortunate in underdeveloped nations, caught the attention of many. Princess Dianna and Heather Mills, Sir Paul McCartney's now ex wife, were avid supporters of the Heart Wheels Foundation that Zlatomir founded to help these children.

He decided he needed to follow the sun and in 2007 he moved to Arizona and he happily lives in Phoenix to this day.

When he left his home country he also left behind his degree in Engineering, but he found a very rewarding job with a company that uses his knowledge and skills to create and build specialized equipment for the disabled and handicapped. In addition, Zlatomir had to learn English when he moved to the United States. While he worked with the handicapped, they found his name too hard to pronounce or remember so his American friends and clients call him "Ze".

Zlatomir hasn't forgotten his terrible time in the war. He deals with the horrible memories of the suffering in the prison camps and on the streets of his home town, by making plans to continue his humanitarian works by donating a portion of the proceeds of his book to institutions that help war veterans in Bosnia, including the many children who continue to be victims of an ungodly war and poverty.

Zlatomir's father gave his last-born son the perfect name. This man has a heart of "Gold" and continues to help others here in the United States who are disabled, through his current job by using his engineering knowledge by creating ways to make the disabled mobile.

www.ingramcontent.com/pod-product-compliance
Lightning Source LLC
Chambersburg PA
CBHW020539290526
45786CB00002B/957